Massachusetts

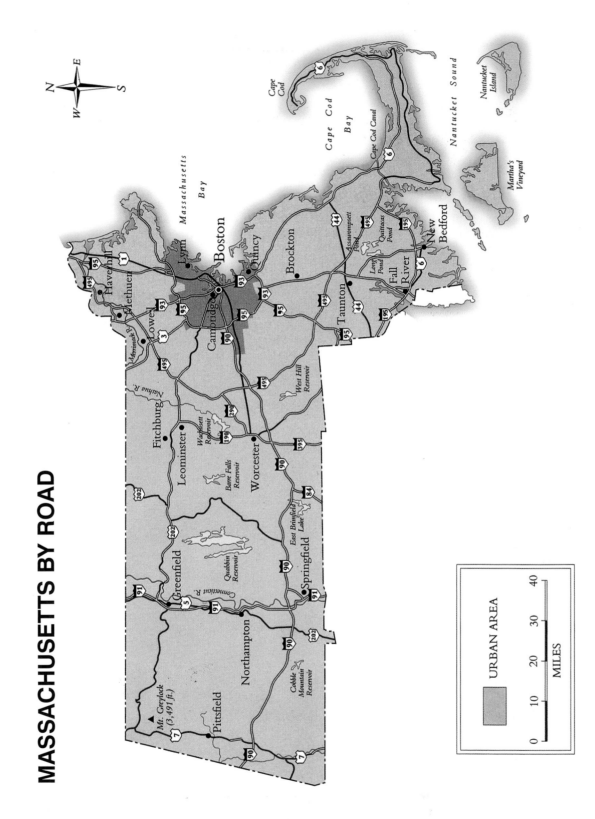

MASSACHUSETTS BY ROAD

N E S W

Cape Cod

Cape Cod Bay

Cape Cod Canal

Nantucket Sound

Nantucket Island

Martha's Vineyard

Massachusetts Bay

Lynn
Boston
Quincy
Brockton
Cambridge
Haverhill
Methuen
Lowell

Taunton
Fall River
New Bedford

Assawompsett Pond
Quittacas Pond
Long Pond

West Hill Reservoir

Fitchburg
Leominster
Worcester
Wachusett Reservoir
Barre Falls Reservoir

East Brimfield Lake
Quabbin Reservoir

Greenfield
Springfield
Northampton
Connecticut R.
Nashua R.
Merrimack R.

Cobble Mountain Reservoir

Mt. Greylock (3,491 ft.)
Pittsfield

95 1 495 93 3 290 190 495 395 90 84 202 91 5 202 90 7 6 44 195 144

URBAN AREA

MILES
0 10 20 30 40

Celebrate the States

Massachusetts

Suzanne LeVert and Tamra B. Orr

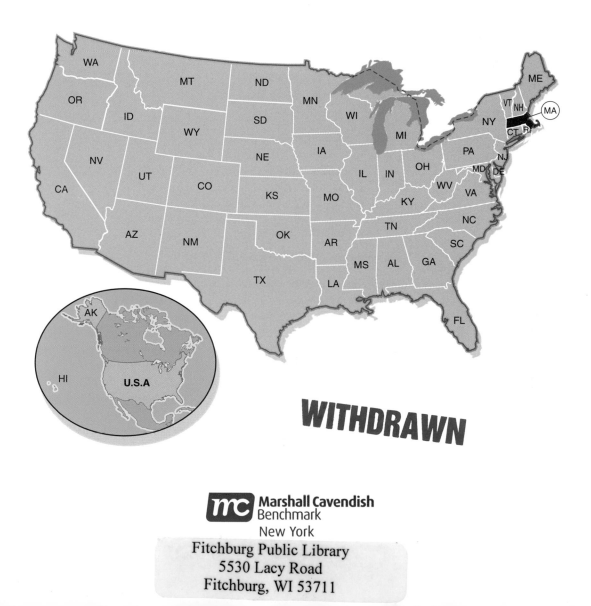

WITHDRAWN

mc **Marshall Cavendish**
Benchmark
New York

Marshall Cavendish Benchmark
99 White Plains Road
Tarrytown, New York 10591-5502
www.marshallcavendish.us

All Internet sites were correct at time of printing.

Library of Congress Cataloging-in-Publication Data
LeVert, Suzanne.
Massachusetts / by Suzanne LeVert and Tamra B. Orr. — 2nd ed.
p. cm. — (Celebrate the states)
Summary: "Provides comprehensive information on the geography, history, wildlife, governmental
structure, economy, cultural diversity, peoples, religion, and landmarks of Massachusetts"—Provided
by publisher.
Includes bibliographical references and index.
ISBN 978-0-7614-3005-6
1. Massachusetts—Juvenile literature. I. Orr, Tamra. II. Title.
F64.3.L48 2008
974.4—dc22
2007035016

Editor: Christine Florie
Contributing Editor: Nikki Bruno Clapper
Publisher: Michelle Bisson
Art Director: Anahid Hamparian
Series Designer: Adam Mietlowski

Photo research by Connie Gardner

Cover photo by Walter Bibikow/JAI/CORBIS

The photographs in this book are used by permission and through the courtesy of:
SuperStock: age footstock, back cover, 100; SuperStock, 63; Gala, 68; Prisma, 106; *Getty Images:*
Michael Eudenbach, 8; Altrendo Nature, 18; Steve Dunwell, 22; Hulton Archive, 34; Getty Images
Sports, 67; Image Bank, 78; Business Wire, 81, 89; Christian Science Monitor, 82; *Alamy:* Andre
Jenny, 14; Eric Fowke, 57; Kim Hackett, 92; Ross Frid, 113 (T); *Corbis:* Rob Howard, 10; Kevin
Flemming, 13, 99, 105; Bill Schermeister, 15; Robert and Lorri Franz, 21; Rick Friedman, 23, 73,
103; The Gallery Collection, 37; Bettmann, 38, 39, 44, 46, 47, 48, 71, 75, 125, 129, 133 (T & B);
Medford Historical Society, 45; Ed Quinn, 50; Paul Buck, 65; Mike Blake, 66; Catherine Karnow,
84; CORBIS, 87, 130; Richard T. Nowitz, 90; James Marshall, 94, 98, 110; David G. Houser, 96;
Reuters, 97; Lee Snider, 102; John L. Simbert, 104; DILLC, 113 (B); *Dembinsky Photo Associates:*
Skip Moody, 16, 17; *Minden Pictures:* Mark Moffett, 117; *North Wind Picture Archives:* 26, 28;
Bridgeman Art Library: Captain John Smith (1580–1631) lst Governor of Virginia c 1818 (oil on
canvas) English School (17th century)/Private Collection; *The Image Works:* ARPL/HIP, 31; Dorothy
Littell/Greco, 52, 59, 108; Marilyn Humphries, 55; Andre Jenny, 95, 101; Mike Evans, 126.

Printed in Malaysia
1 3 5 6 4 2

Contents

Massachusetts Is . . .

Massachusetts is the cradle of liberty.

"Behold [Massachusetts], and judge for yourselves. There is her history; the world knows it by heart. The past, at least, is secure. There is Boston, and Concord, and Lexington, and Bunker Hill; and there they will remain forever. The bones of her sons, fallen in the great struggle for Independence, now lie mingled with the soil of every state from New England to Georgia, and there they will lie forever."
> —Daniel Webster, eighteenth-century statesman

"[Massachusetts] was the first in the war of Independence, first to break the chains of her slaves; first to make the black man equal before the law; first to admit colored children to her common school."
> —Frederick Douglass, antislavery activist

"Maybe it's how close we are to history here that makes Massachusetts such an interesting place to write about, or the sense that this was the initial American frontier, or the literary legacy of so many great Massachusetts writers."
> —Alice Hoffman, author

The state is home to a singular population.

"Only Bostonians can understand Bostonians."
> —Henry Adams, historian

"The people of Massachusetts are so proud, so optimistic, so practical, so hopeful. A people of ingenuity and drive and grit and determination.

A people of fundamental civility and warmth. A people from a tradition of high standards and high expectations. This is the character of the people of Massachusetts."

—Patrick Duval, governor

Massachusetts is also home to Boston, a unique capital city.

"Boston is a state of mind."

—Mark Twain, author

"Boston is known for its innovation."

—Thomas M. Menino, mayor of Boston

"I played before the greatest fans in baseball, the Boston fans."

—Ted Williams, baseball player

"Boston is an oasis in the desert, a place where the larger proportion of people are loving, rational and happy."

—Julia Ward Howe, activist

Finally, Massachusetts is filled with promise for the future.

"This city is like 350 years of history with a future."

—James Koch, Boston entrepreneur

The birthplace of the United States, the high-tech capital of the East, the home of the Red Sox and the Patriots—Massachusetts has a history, a landscape, and a spirit all its own. In the pages that follow, you'll learn how the past meets the future in Boston. You'll see where the power of the sea meets the granite shore to create the stark landscape of Cape Ann. You'll also meet some of the people who make up this state's diverse, hardworking population. Indeed, Massachusetts has much to boast about as it enters the twenty-first century.

Chapter One

A Paradise by the Sea

Tucked into the middle of New England is Massachusetts, also known as the Bay State. One of the country's smallest states, Massachusetts is incredibly diverse. Its long, rectangular shape changes drastically as it reaches the Atlantic Ocean to the east. Here the state stops abruptly at a ragged edge with a downward-facing hook that looks like a beckoning finger. "Come and explore my mysteries," the land seems to say. Although the state is little, there is a great deal to see, to enjoy, and to appreciate.

Massachusetts earned its nickname because there is a large bay along its eastern shore. The state lies in the northeastern corner of the United States. Every other New England state except Maine borders Massachusetts—Vermont and New Hampshire to the north, Rhode Island and Connecticut to the south. New York, which is not part of New England, forms the state's western border.

Massachusetts is small. In fact, seventy states the size of Massachusetts would fit inside Alaska, the largest U.S. state. What the Bay State

The Gay Head Lighthouse in Aquinnah sits atop the 130-foot multicolored clay cliffs on the western side of Martha's Vineyard.

lacks in size, however, it makes up for with its great variety of landscapes. While 60 percent of Massachusetts is forested, the state also boasts snow-peaked mountains, sand dunes, and rocky shorelines.

RIVERS, VALLEYS, AND SEASHORES

The seacoast forms an essential part of the Massachusetts landscape. Beaches and sand dunes line Massachusetts Bay and the fishhook-shaped peninsula of Cape Cod, which sticks out into the Atlantic Ocean. On one side of the peninsula is Cape Cod Bay. On the other is Nantucket Sound, which harbors Martha's Vineyard and Nantucket Island. These two islands offer windswept beaches and quaint villages to thousands of year-round residents and hundreds of thousands of tourists each summer.

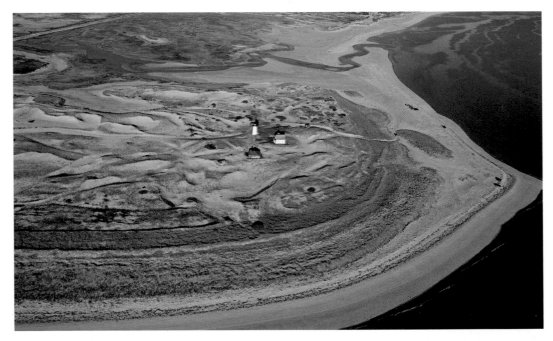

This aerial photograph shows Cape Cod's Race Point. Its name came from the strong crosscurrent that made the shore a nightmare for sailors.

LAND AND WATER

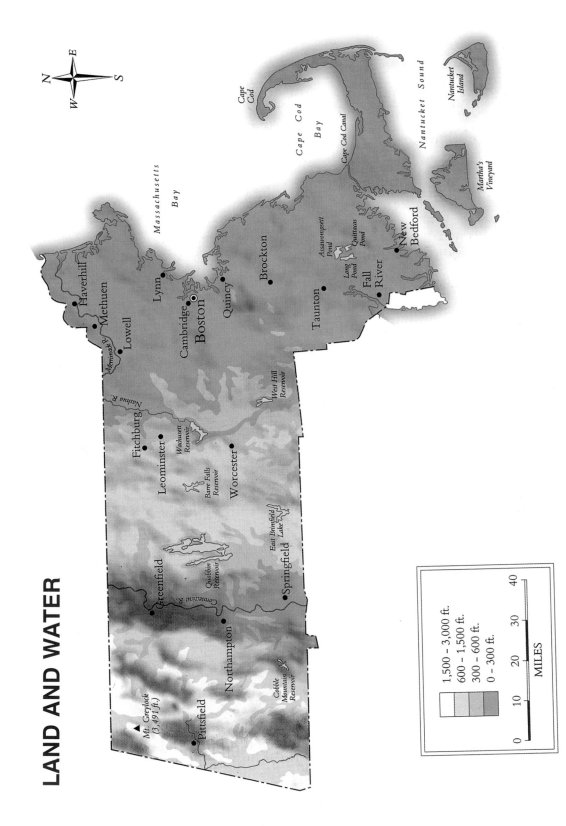

Mt. Greylock
(3,491 ft.)

Pittsfield

Northampton

Greenfield

Connecticut R.

Quabbin Reservoir

Cobble Mountain Reservoir

Springfield

East Brinfield Lake

Worcester

Barre Falls Reservoir

Leominster

Wachusett Reservoir

Fitchburg

Nashua R.

West Hill Reservoir

Lowell

Merrimack R.

Haverhill

Methuen

Lynn

Cambridge

Boston

Quincy

Brockton

Taunton

Fall River

New Bedford

Long Pond

Assawompsett Pond

Quittacas Pond

Massachusetts Bay

Cape Cod

Cape Cod Bay

Cape Cod Canal

Nantucket Sound

Nantucket Island

Martha's Vineyard

N
E
S
W

	1,500 – 3,000 ft.
	600 – 1,500 ft.
	300 – 600 ft.
	0 – 300 ft.

0   10   20   30   40
MILES

The Massachusetts coastline measures 192 miles from its northern boundary at New Hampshire to its southern border at Rhode Island. If the coastline of each bay and inlet were added to the total, however, the state's coastline would measure 1,900 miles—more than the coast of California. The Massachusetts coast is extremely varied. "I spend as many summer weekends as possible on Cape Ann to the north of Boston, while friends of mine would rather stay in Cape Cod to the south," remarks Roz Kramer, a Boston resident who prefers the north's rocky shoreline to the south's long stretches of sandy seashore.

Some of the state's largest rivers, including the Merrimack, the Mystic, and the Charles, flow east into the bays. These rivers helped make harbor cities such as Boston, Gloucester, Weymouth, New Bedford, and Fall River important fishing and transportation centers.

THE CREATION OF THE ISLANDS: A WAMPANOAG MYTH

According to the Wampanoag people, Martha's Vineyard and Nantucket Island were created by a great giant named Moshop. Moshop was so big that he used the whole length of Cape Cod's beaches as a bed. Because strange visions came to Moshop in his dreams, he tossed and turned as he slept. One night, his restless movements filled his moccasins with sand and made them heavy. Half asleep, he kicked one moccasin a short distance into the sea. Then he kicked the other shoe farther out toward the horizon. The first moccasin became the island of Noepe—Martha's Vineyard—and the second became the island of Natockete, or Nantucket.

The Longfellow Bridge, which connects Boston and Cambridge, stretches out over the Charles River.

Central Massachusetts features fertile valleys dotted with marigolds and azaleas. Birch, pine, and beech trees fill the forests. Within this area is Worcester, a commercial city whose residents once used the rushing Blackstone River to power the city's many textile mills and other industries. The little town of Webster has a lake with the longest name in the world: Lake Chargoggagoggmanchaugagoggchaubunagungamaug, which means, "You fish your side of the lake. I fish my side. Nobody fishes in the middle." A Webster resident remarks, "We just call it Lake Webster, its other name. It's easier that way, don't you think?"

The Connecticut River, the longest river in New England, runs north to south through the center of Massachusetts. The rolling hills and valleys near the river are speckled with delicate violets and other wildflowers every spring. The rich, reddish-brown soil here makes the Connecticut River valley the state's most important agricultural region. Farmers in the valley grow fruit and corn and raise livestock. "I love driving through this area," a salesman from Boston remarks, "especially in the summer when the crops are growing and the cornstalks are so tall. You're really in the middle of the country, but yet you're less than a hundred miles from Boston."

West of this region, the land gets increasingly hilly. The Berkshire Hills is a landscape of high peaks, lush valleys, and cool mountain streams. This region includes Mount Greylock. At 3,491 feet above sea level, Greylock's peak is the highest spot in Massachusetts.

The Connecticut River valley is the Bay State's main agricultural region.

Monument Mountain, in the Berkshire Hills, was a favorite hiking spot of famous authors Nathaniel Hawthorne, Oliver Wendell Holmes, and Herman Melville.

WHERE THE WILD THINGS ARE

The forests of Massachusetts are filled with foxes, muskrats, porcupines, rabbits, chipmunks, red and gray squirrels, raccoons, and striped skunks. White-tailed deer dart behind trees, and bobcats slink along in the shadows watching for their next meals. The meadow mouse is the state's most common animal. Many beavers live in the state's streams, while river otters spend their days playing in the water. Poisonous snakes, such as northern copperheads and timber rattlesnakes, slither through the woods.

Framed by New England asters, a chipmunk fills its cheeks with food.

Massachusetts is home to more than 330 species of birds. Overhead you can see cardinals, bald eagles, owls, and plenty of chickadees, the state bird. Seagulls fly near the coast by the thousands. Mallard ducks fill the sky with their honking cries, while woodpeckers add a tap-tap-tap rhythm to the forests. "Williamstown, in the Berkshires, is one of my favorite places to vacation," remarks a California native who spends every September in New England. "There is such a variety of species of wildlife, and the landscape is so inviting, especially in the fall when the leaves change."

A black-capped chickadee, the state bird of Massachusetts, perches on a branch of milkweed.

The state's lakes and ponds are filled with bass, pickerel, trout, and white and yellow perch. Along the shores you can find red-spotted newts, salamanders, toads, and frogs. You might even spot a snapping turtle or two. In the coastal waters are clams, oysters, lobsters, mussels, shrimp, crabs, and many varieties of fish—haddock, flounder, tuna, and herring. You can also find some cod, which used to exist in great abundance. A wooden carving of this fish, called the Sacred Cod, hangs in the Massachusetts State House today in honor of the bounty that drew settlers to the area by the thousands.

Maidenhair ferns, lilies, orchids, and goldenrod are found throughout the state, along with a rainbow of wildflowers like the blue flag and the New England aster. The butterfly weed grows up to 3 feet tall and has bright pink, snapdragonlike flowers that attract butterflies. The crimson red cardinal flower provides nectar for the state's hummingbirds.

A bright field of goldenrod is a familiar sight in many parts of Massachusetts.

THE RIGHT WHALE

If you've ever seen one, you know that few creatures are as magnificent as the whale. Highly intelligent, graceful despite their size, and almost friendly in the way they often travel alongside ships at sea, whales have long fascinated people. Some whales, including the right whale, are among the world's endangered species. Current estimates indicate that no more than three hundred northern right whales are left on Earth.

Beginning eight hundred years ago and lasting well into the twentieth century, right whales were hunted extensively, primarily for their oil and baleen (hornlike plates in the whale's jaw that were used to make serving platters and utensils). The animal's valuable oil, slow swimming speed, and abundance along the coasts combined to make it the "right" whale to kill. So many right whales were slaughtered that their population has not recovered, despite more than fifty years of efforts to protect the species.

Northern right whales spend spring and summer off the coast of New England, and late summer and fall in waters off southern Canada. Although the whales are no longer hunted, they continue to face danger from humans. Some collide with ships, others get tangled up in fishing gear, and many live in polluted waters. Whale-watching tours from New Bedford, Gloucester, and Boston are popular, but few people see right whales. Only twenty reliable sightings have been reported since 1900.

Some of the animals in Massachusetts have become endangered or even extinct. At least seven species that once thrived in the state, including the eastern elk and the passenger pigeon, are no longer found anywhere in the world. More than seventy other species, including the lynx and the eastern gray wolf, no longer live in Massachusetts. The state does, however, host a significant population of endangered birds, including the roseate tern and the piping plover. Despite efforts to protect the piping plover, only about five thousand survive today. Just four hundred make their nests in Massachusetts.

Other endangered animals in the state include the puma, several species of sea turtles, and five species of whales. In 2004, the state passed the Massachusetts Endangered Species Act, which outlines species that are considered threatened or endangered and states punishments for anyone attempting to capture, transport, export, sell, or buy any of these creatures. The act also prohibits people from changing or interfering with endangered species' habitats. According to the act, breaking either of these laws would result in fines of up to $10,000 or imprisonment for up to three months.

Some of the species listed on the Bay State's endangered list are plants that are becoming increasingly hard to find. For example, the sandplain gerardia is becoming much rarer. Sandplain gerardia has fragile pink blossoms.

THE CHANGING SEASONS

"If you don't like the weather in New England, just wait a few minutes," humorist Ring Lardner once said. Many Massachusetts residents have borrowed this quotation when attempting to describe the state's constantly changing climate. Like its geography, the weather of Massachusetts

The piping plover is an endangered species, but several birds live and breed in Massachusetts.

never fails to offer variety, and lots of it—sun, rain, snow, sleet, hail, thunderstorms, and hurricanes.

Throughout the state, summers can be hot and humid. Heat waves of 90 degrees Fahrenheit and above happen regularly, especially during August. Thanks to the state's plentiful lakes and oceanfront, most residents find relief easy to come by. "We hardly ever need an air conditioner," says John Fitzgerald, a lifelong resident of Rockport. "The breeze from the ocean, along with a few well-placed fans, is all we need."

People from all over the country—even the world—flock to Massachusetts to experience the crisp fall days and colorful foliage. October is particularly spectacular, with its clear blue skies, moderate temperatures, and splashes of red, orange, and yellow leaves.

Winter, though, is a different story. The winters are fairly long, sometimes lasting from November to early April. Temperatures average about 31 °F—just cold enough for snow. In the western part of the state, the average snowfall is 55 to 75 inches a year. This number decreases in the eastern sections of Massachusetts. In 1978, an infamous blizzard broke all-time snowfall records. The storm dropped 4 feet of snow in 32 hours.

The vibrant colors of autumn are reflected in the waters of Laurel Lake in the Berkshire Hills.

New Englanders must be on the alert for more than thirty nor'easters that track up the Atlantic seaboard from December to March every year. Nor'easters are similar to hurricanes, but they tend to last longer. "The big nor'easter of 1978 was nothing like I'd ever seen," remarks a resident of Cape Ann. "The snow piled up faster than you can imagine, and the wind was so cold. But it was the power of the sea, churned up by the wind, that was most amazing. Slabs of granite 2,000 pounds heavy were thrown by the waves. This one storm changed the face of the coastline forever."

A Boston resident walks past buried cars after a blizzard in December 2003.

The Blackstone River, which flows from Worcester, Massachusetts, to Providence, Rhode Island, was the first polluted river in the United States. A cotton-spinning operation named Slater Mill, the nation's first water-powered textile mill, was the source of the pollution. Throughout the nineteenth century, residents complained that the river was making them ill. The Blackstone was so foul that textile mills had to find other sources of water to wash their wool. Pollution continued to devastate this and other waterways throughout the state for another hundred years.

The Clean Water Act, passed by Congress in 1972, addressed water pollution by setting cleanliness standards and providing funds to help the states clean up their rivers, lakes, and harbors. With federal and state help, the Blackstone is now a source of pride. In 1995, U.S. secretary of the interior Bruce Babbitt went to the banks of the Blackstone and declared, "The wonderful story is that this river—the first truly polluted river in America, the cradle of the Industrial Revolution—now becomes the cradle of another opportunity, the cradle of revival and renewal."

One of the most difficult challenges facing Massachusetts has been cleaning up its harbors. Harbors in Gloucester, Salem, and New Bedford were convenient spots to dispose of human and industrial waste. Indeed, much more than tea has been dumped in Boston Harbor, the state's largest port, which once was considered the most polluted harbor in the nation.

Around 1950, Boston built two sewage treatment plants, but they weren't big enough to handle all the city's sewage. By the 1970s, more than 500 million gallons of poorly treated wastewater was flowing into the harbor every day. By 1984, harbor fish had become poisonous, and more than 15,000 fishing-industry workers had lost their jobs.

In response to this problem, state officials upgraded the old treatment plants and built new ones. Today, the water in Boston Harbor is much cleaner. Its beaches are now safe for swimming, and marine life such as porpoises and seals is returning. The thirty-four-island Boston Harbor Islands National Park attracts locals and tourists alike with its shell-covered beaches, hiking paths, historical forts, and fields of berries. Each island has something unique to offer, from a Civil War fort on George's Island to old stone farmhouses on Bumpkin Island.

Today, many Massachusetts citizens take environmental problems to heart and work together to prevent them. This approach helped save Grazing Field Farm in southern Massachusetts. The family that owned the 900-acre farm cultivated only 50 acres of it. The rest was left in its natural state and was populated by birds and other wildlife that lived in its wetlands. When the state planned to build a highway across the farm, the community gathered to protest. The battle over the highway—which the citizens won—led Massachusetts to pass the Wetlands Protection Act, which now serves as a model for other state leaders who want to pass similar protection laws. This spirit of community and social change has been a mainstay of Massachusetts throughout its history.

For the past nineteen years, the Massachusetts Office of Coastal Management has organized thousands of volunteers, from retirees to students, for its annual Coastsweep. Volunteers help clean hundreds of miles of shoreline and riverbanks. They even put on scuba-diving equipment and clean up parts of the ocean floor. In 2006, one fifty-person team working to clean up Wollaston Beach in Quincy picked up thirty bags of trash containing 1,384 cigarette butts. All in all, 3,077 people participated in Coastsweep 2006. They collected 38,466 pounds of trash from almost 150 miles of shoreline.

Chapter Two

The City upon the Hill

When you think about the first people to live in Massachusetts, you might imagine the Pilgrims. The first people in the region were actually a group known as Paleo-Indians, the ancestors of Native Americans, who arrived up to ten thousand years ago. Paleo-Indians lived in small groups and spent their days fishing, hunting, and gathering food. Over thousands of years, their numbers grew and their culture developed. They learned how to farm and to create tools out of stone and wood. They built homes, wove baskets, sewed leather, and carved out canoes. By the time the first Europeans settlers traveled to New England, these tribes had lived in the area for more than a hundred centuries.

NATIVE AMERICANS

By about 5000 BCE, some Paleo-Indians had settled in small communities near what is now Plymouth. They survived by hunting, gathering fruit, and fishing. They lived in relative peace until Algonquian Native-American tribes drove them out in about 2000 BCE. The Algonquian tribes set up permanent villages throughout North America. Tribes that settled in

The Puritans were a prominent group in early Massachusetts history. This young Puritan woman reads as she spins.

Massachusetts included the Nauset, Nipmuc, Pocomtuc, Wampanoag, and Patuxet. The tribe that gave the state its name—the Massachusetts, which means "near the great hill"—lived near present-day Boston, from Salem to Quincy.

The Native Americans of Massachusetts lived in dome-shaped huts called wigwams, built of bark, dry grass, and tree branches. Each family cooked on a fire pit in the wigwam; a hole in the roof served as a chimney. They fished, hunted, and farmed. Groups traveled from place to place by walking or canoeing. Some of the tribespeople wore beaded and feathered headbands, and almost all people wore moccasins. Men usually shaved their heads or wore one long strip of hair, called a scalplock, on top of their heads. They decorated their bodies with tattoos. While the native peoples of Massachusetts were at peace with many tribes, such as the Mohican and the Delaware, they fought battles with the Iroquois.

Wampanoag warriors were imposing figures. European explorers noted, "They exceed us in size."

One legend said that a giant named Moshup once lived on the Massachusetts shoreline. One day, Moshup decided to settle down on the island of Martha's Vineyard. He would sit on top of a hill near Gay Head (his seat can still be seen today in the crater above the cliffs). The giant caught whales with his hands and cooked them over the forest's trees. That is why Gay Head has so few trees left today. Moshup shared his whale meat with the native people, and to show their appreciation, they gave him an entire harvest of tobacco. Moshup put it in his pipe and smoked it. He dumped the ashes into the water, and the ashes created Nantucket Island. One day, Moshup warned the tribes that dangerous, fair-skinned men were on their way, and the Native Americans should not allow them on shore. He slipped into the water to wait and see what would happen next. After the tribes greeted the white men and allowed them to stay, Moshup was never seen again.

EUROPEANS EXPLORE

At one time, at least 30,000 Native Americans lived in the Massachusetts area. By the time the Pilgrims arrived in 1620, only about seven thousand Native Americans remained. The others had died of diseases brought by the earliest European explorers.

Most likely, the first European to see the Massachusetts coast was John Cabot, who arrived in 1498 and claimed the land for England. Many historians think that the first Europeans to go ashore were led by Portuguese sailor Miguel Corte-Real in 1502. According to some accounts, Corte-Real and his crew lived with the local Native Americans for at least nine years after being shipwrecked.

By 1602, profit-minded English merchants sent Bartholomew Gosnold to the New England region in search of sassafras, a tree with a root used for flavoring foods and soups and making medicinal potions. Instead, Gosnold found so many cod swimming in the waters that he named the spot Cape Cod. On the same voyage, he landed at an island that he named Martha's Vineyard after his daughter. Twelve years later, English sea captain John Smith mapped the coastline north of Cape Cod Bay. He called the area New England.

Captain John Smith was famous among the colonists of New England.

THE PILGRIMS ARRIVE

In the early 1600s, a group of English Protestants wanted to separate from the powerful Church of England. They wanted to practice religion in their own way but were not allowed to do so in England. After reading John Smith's description of the beauty and economic potential of Massachusetts, they decided to start a church in this new land.

On September 16, 1620, 102 people seeking religious freedom set sail from Plymouth, England, toward North America on a ship named the *Mayflower*. After sixty-five stormy days, the exhausted and frightened settlers landed at present-day Provincetown. The view of the wilderness from the small ship was gloomy. One passenger, William Bradford, wrote, "The whole country, full of woods and thickets, represented a wild and savage hue." According to some accounts, Bradford's wife, Dorothy, was so overcome with dread that she threw herself overboard and drowned.

Pilgrims board the Mayflower *for their 3,000-mile voyage from England to North America.*

Nevertheless, the majority of the passengers were committed to making a new life in this new land. Before leaving the ship, they drew up a form of self-government that they called the Mayflower Compact. This was the first time British colonists saw themselves as a political body with the right to create their own laws and style of government. In December, the group sailed across Cape Cod Bay and settled in Plymouth.

To the Pilgrims' surprise, they found much of the area abandoned, rather than full of the Native Americans they had been told about. The native people were not hiding, however. An incredible number had died because of the diseases brought over by Europeans. Without any immunity to illnesses like small pox, it did not take long for an epidemic to begin. In some places, up to 90 percent of the Native Americans died.

THE FIRST THANKSGIVING

The Pilgrims' first winter in Massachusetts was brutal, and many died of the same diseases that had devastated the native tribes. In March 1621, one colonist wrote, "Dies Elizabeth, wife of Mr. Edward Winslow. This month thirteen of our number die. . . . Of a hundred persons, scarce fifty remain, the living scarce able to bury the dead." The rest might also have died if not for the help of the Native Americans. A Patuxet man named Squanto taught the Pilgrims more efficient ways to fish, to hunt, to plant, and to cook in their new land.

By the following fall, the colony was self-sufficient, and the settlers observed their first Thanksgiving. For three days the Pilgrims feasted with the Native Americans. They thanked God—and their native neighbors—for delivering them from hunger and hardship. More settlers arrived in Plymouth Colony during the years that followed, and by 1640 the colony had eight towns and 25,000 people.

THE PURITANS

While Plymouth Colony was growing, a second English colony had begun in Massachusetts. The members of this colony still belonged to the Church of England, but they wanted to simplify and purify its beliefs and practices. Calling themselves Puritans, these settlers started the Massachusetts Bay Colony. Some arrived in Salem in 1629. Boston, the colony's main town, began in 1630. The Puritans thought their community would serve as a model for the rest of the world. "We must consider that we shall be a city upon a hill, the eyes of all people upon us," said the colony's leader, John Winthrop.

The Puritan way of life was serious and somewhat harsh. Puritan leaders saw human nature as sinful, and they thought acts such as dancing and singing were invitations from the devil. Even the celebration of Christmas was outlawed in Puritan colonies until 1681. An edict proclaimed, "Whosoever shall be found observing any such day as Christmas or the like . . . shall pay for every such offense five shillings." The Puritans lived by a strict moral code. They had little tolerance for people who believed otherwise, and even less tolerance for people who lived otherwise. Although they banned all religions besides their own, the Puritans established political freedom and a form of government based on elected representatives as voices of the people—traditions still held dear in Massachusetts today.

As the two colonies grew, relations among Native Americans and colonists became strained. The Native Americans knew they were slowly being pushed off their land. A Wampanoag leader named Metacom, also called King Philip, became angry and tried to drive out the settlers. In 1675 and 1676, he and his warriors fought King Philip's War. However, Metacom's fighters were no match for the settlers, who had much greater numbers.

Metacom, known also as King Philip, was the leader of King Philip's War, one of the deadliest and most expensive wars in U.S. history.

In 1691, Plymouth Colony and Massachusetts Bay Colony joined to form Massachusetts Colony, which grew rapidly in the years that followed. By 1750, Massachusetts had a population of 200,000.

TRIAL BY FIRE: THE SALEM WITCH HUNT

In 1692, Salem Village was a quiet Puritan community—that is, until strange forces seemed to take over a group of young women. Nine-year-old Elizabeth Parris, daughter of Reverend Samuel Parris, and her eleven-year-old cousin began to have fits of convulsions. The girls claimed that an invisible hand was pinching them and leaving red marks all over their bodies. When Samuel Parris insisted that the children explain their demonic possession, the girls accused three townswomen of casting spells on them.

The village erupted in panic as Parris and his followers accused most of the town's outcasts of witchcraft. Even the wife of William Phips, governor of the colony, came under suspicion. A special court in Salem convicted nineteen people as witches and executed them. Giles Corey, who had testified against his wife, Martha, was pressed to death with heavy stones when he would not confess to being a witch. "More weight, more weight," was all Corey could manage to say as he died. In total, 150 people went to jail for witchcraft. Slowly, the Salem colonists returned to their senses, and Governor Phips ended the trials and released all those imprisoned for witchcraft.

By this time, the economy of Massachusetts was thriving. It had a robust shipbuilding industry, and its merchants were making a lot of money in overseas trade. Merchants shipped dried fish, corn, salt, and lumber to the West Indies in exchange for cotton, dyes, tobacco, and molasses.

Meanwhile, England engaged in what became known as the French and Indian War. After fighting France for the land of North America, England emerged victorious—but poor—in 1763. England was so desperate for money that it began taxing the colonists to raise funds. The first direct tax imposed on the American colonies was the Stamp Act of 1765. This placed a tax on printed materials such as contracts, newspapers, pamphlets, and even playing cards.

Enraged colonists immediately formed a group called the Sons of Liberty to oppose the Stamp Act. They did so not only because they didn't want to pay the tax, but also because they had no representatives and no vote in the British parliament. In the eyes of the colonists, no vote should have meant no tax. They protested with the slogan "No taxation without representation."

On December 16, 1773, the Sons of Liberty held a protest against the British government's tax on tea. They dressed up as Native Americans and dumped 342 chests of British tea into Boston Harbor. This event, dubbed the Boston Tea Party, outraged the British. They sent troops to blockade Boston Harbor, and they stripped the colonists of their right to appoint judges and juries. Tensions mounted with each passing day. Following the Boston Tea Party, future president John Adams wrote, "Now the die is cast. The people have crossed the river and cut away the bridge! Last night three cargoes of tea were emptied into the harbor. This is the grandest event which has ever yet happened since the controversy with Britain opened!"

During the Boston Tea Party, two hundred men whooped war chants as they dumped British tea into Boston Harbor.

As news of the events in Boston spread throughout the colonies, the seeds of revolution were planted. Throughout Massachusetts, people began stockpiling guns and ammunition in case the British used force. The citizen soldiers called themselves minutemen. They boasted that they could be ready for action at a minute's notice.

In April 1775, British soldiers, who were called Redcoats because of their bright red uniforms, were spotted heading toward the towns of Lexington and Concord, where colonists had stored large amounts of weapons. That night, Paul Revere and others took their famous midnight horseback ride to warn the two towns. As a result, by the time the Redcoats arrived, the minutemen were waiting. In this first battle of the Revolutionary War, about 20 percent of Britain's soldiers were killed, wounded, or missing—perhaps because their bright red coats made excellent targets.

After the battles of Lexington and Concord, a British general wrote, "A few more such victories would have surely put an end to British dominion in America."

One of the most famous battles of the American Revolution was the Battle of Bunker Hill in June 1775. In this battle, the British lost nearly half their men. This turn of events boosted the confidence of the colonial soldiers. Less than one year later, colonial troops led by George Washington forced the British out of Boston forever. Battles continued, but finally the British and the Americans signed a peace treaty in 1783. All British soldiers were withdrawn from the colonies. The Americans were now free from British rule.

ATTUCKS ATTACKS: THE BOSTON MASSACRE

On the early evening of March 5, 1770, a lone Redcoat stood at his post, minding his business. To many Bostonians, however, he represented the British abuse of the colonies. The colonists were angry and tired of living under Britain's thumb. The presence of Redcoats felt like a grip around their throats. A small group of men gathered to taunt this lone Redcoat with jeers and snowballs.

The news of the brewing trouble quickly reached British soldiers stationed in nearby barracks. As the soldiers arrived, so did more angry townspeople. One colonist, Crispus Attucks, rounded up some men who wielded clubs and weapons. Attucks was a powerful man who was about 6 feet tall. Historians say he was probably either an African American or a full-blooded member of the Natick tribe, though his true ethnic background remains in question.

A small squad of British soldiers was ordered to load their muskets but not to fire. Overwhelmed by the snowballs, rocks, and insults thrown at them, the Redcoats began firing into the crowd anyway. Eleven colonists were hit by bullets, and five died. Among the dead lay Crispus Attucks, the first person to die in the American fight for freedom. A Massachusetts patriot named Samuel Adams dubbed the event the Boston Massacre.

Many Americans forget that there were two sides participating in the Boston Massacre. Samuel Adams's cousin, John Adams, did not forget. John, who was a lawyer, believed in fair trials. He successfully defended the British soldiers in court.

YANKEE INGENUITY

As the young country grew, so did the shipping and trading business in Massachusetts. Soon, however, tensions again arose between the United States and Britain, and the two nations went to war. The War of 1812 prevented Massachusetts from buying goods from Europe, and the state was forced to make its own products. Workers adapted well, and Massachusetts soon led the young nation in manufacturing. The state's "can-do" mentality became known as Yankee ingenuity.

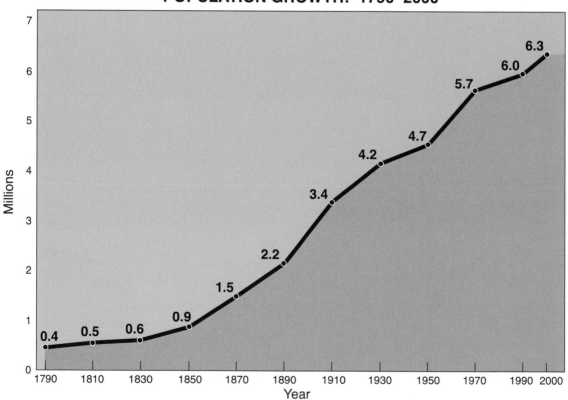

POPULATION GROWTH: 1790–2000

The first half of the nineteenth century was prosperous for Massachusetts. Farming communities sprang up in the Berkshire valleys, while toll roads, canals, and railroads were built along the rivers. In 1814, businessman Francis Cabot Lowell built a cotton mill in the town of Waltham. This mill was the first in the United States to turn raw cotton into finished cloth. After Lowell's death, his partners built an entire city filled with mills on the banks of the Merrimack River and named it Lowell. Companies in Lowell made clothing, furniture, musical instruments, and clipper ships.

As the state's economy grew, European immigrants arrived to look for jobs. Between 1846 and 1856, more than a thousand Irish newcomers settled in Boston each month. Bay Staters of English descent discriminated against the newcomers at first, but the Irish eventually gained respect in the political and economic arenas. In the 1880s, John Breen and Hugh O'Brien became the first Irish mayors of Lawrence and Boston respectively. In 1892, upon his election to the state senate, Patrick Joseph Kennedy became the first in a long line of Kennedys to hold political office.

NEW IDEAS

With the arrival of new people came new ways of thinking. A new religious movement called Unitarianism developed in Massachusetts. In sharp contrast to Puritans, Unitarians believed in the ultimate goodness of the human spirit. Many Unitarians practiced social reform by helping to improve working conditions and fighting for higher wages for factory workers.

During this period, Massachusetts citizens fought to change many other social issues. Massachusetts native Horace Mann worked tirelessly to improve the nation's schools. Dorothea Dix, who lived most of her life in the Bay State, led the fight for better treatment of the nation's mentally ill people.

BREAD AND ROSES

On January 12, 1912, textile workers in Lawrence, Massachusetts, began a strike that shook the very foundations of the Bay State. The Massachusetts legislature had passed a law limiting the working hours of children under age eighteen to fifty-four hours a week. To get revenge, the textile companies cut the hours of *all* employees to fifty-four hours a week, while also cutting wages. Women were hit particularly hard because their wages were much lower than those of their male coworkers.

During a march through Lawrence, a group of women carried banners proclaiming BREAD AND ROSES! This demand for equal pay for equal work, together with special consideration as women, echoed throughout the country.

Words by James Oppenheim **Music by Martha Coleman**

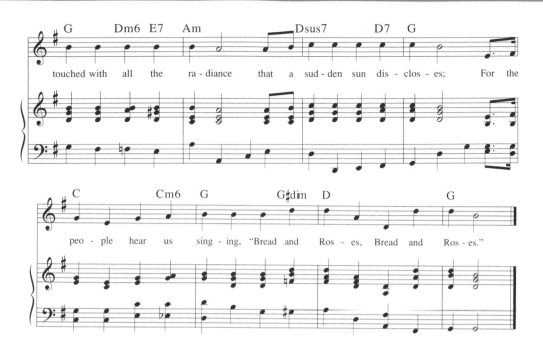

As we come marching, marching, we battle, too, for men,
For they are women's children and we mother them again.
Our lives shall not be sweated from birth until life closes.
Hearts starve as well as bodies:
Give us bread—but give us roses.

As we come marching, marching, unnumbered women dead
Go crying through our singing their ancient song of bread.
Small art and love and beauty their drudging spirit knew.
Yes, it is bread that we fight for,
But we fight for roses, too.

As we come marching, marching, we bring the Greater Days.
The rising of the women means the rising of the race.
No more the drudge and idler—ten that toil where one reposes,
But a sharing of life's glories:
Bread and Roses, Bread and Roses.

Two Massachusetts-born women, Lucy Stone and Susan B. Anthony, helped secure women's right to vote.

The newly developed newspaper and book publishing industry in Massachusetts helped spread new ideas, particularly regarding slavery, throughout the nation. As a result of two 1783 court cases, Massachusetts became the first state to abolish slavery. After that, a strong antislavery movement developed across the state. This trend spread after 1831, when William Lloyd Garrison began publishing the *Liberator,* a newspaper that called for an end to slavery. Garrison also founded the American Anti-Slavery Society.

In 1861, the Civil War broke out between the Southern slaveholding states and the Northern free states. Massachusetts eventually sent nearly 150,000 men into service for the Union. The North's industries were an important part of the war effort. Massachusetts supplied the Union army with guns, blankets, and tents. The Confederacy surrendered in 1865, and slavery was abolished throughout the nation.

Lucy Stone (1818–1893) founded the American Woman Suffrage Association and organized the first national women's rights convention in Worcester.

Officers of a Massachusetts infantry regiment sit for a photograph during the Civil War.

INTO THE TWENTIETH CENTURY

After the Civil War, immigrants poured into Massachusetts in search of work in the state's shipbuilding, textile, and shoemaking factories. Many thousands traveled from Ireland, Italy, Portugal, Germany, and Poland. By 1900 about 30 percent of the population of Massachusetts was foreign-born, and by 1920, foreign-born residents and their children made up 67 percent of the population.

After the United States entered World War I in 1917, factories in Massachusetts manufactured supplies for the U.S. armed forces. Following the war, however, many industries left the state to find cheaper labor down south. By the time the worldwide economic crisis called the Great Depression hit in 1929, Massachusetts was already in financial trouble.

During the Great Depression, hundreds of unemployed workers demand help from the government while marching on Boston Common.

Conditions only worsened as companies and banks went out of business. In the worst years of the Great Depression, almost half the workers in Massachusetts were jobless.

Conditions did not improve until the United States entered World War II in 1941. The factories came alive once again. Massachusetts became a leading producer of war materials, including machinery, radar and sonar technology, and jet engines.

RACE RELATIONS

Although African Americans had lived in Massachusetts for a long time, the state's black population surged after World War II, when tens of thousands of African Americans migrated north from the rural South. Most newcomers settled in and around Boston, where they found themselves at the bottom of the social ladder. African Americans were segregated, or separated, from white society. Visiting Boston in 1965, civil rights leader Martin Luther King Jr. remarked, "I would be dishonest to say that Boston is Birmingham, or that Massachusetts is Mississippi. But it would be irresponsible of me to deny the crippling poverty and the injustice that exist in some sections of this community. . . . Boston must become a testing ground for the ideals of freedom. . . . This fight is not for the sake of the Negro alone, but rather for the aspirations of America itself."

The government passed laws to encourage integration. In 1957, the state legislature prohibited segregation in public housing. Bay Stater Edward Brooke did what he could to improve race relations. In 1966, he became the first African American to win a seat in the U.S. Senate in almost one hundred years. By 1974, as a result of a court order, Boston's public schools were desegregated. Students were bused from one neighborhood to another so that the schools would be racially balanced. This decision sparked years of turmoil.

While serving in the Senate, Edward Brooke investigated the causes of race riots in American cities.

In September 1974, on the third day of court-ordered busing, students are bused back to Roxbury from South Boston under police guard.

In the 1950s and 1960s, the age of computers was dawning in the Bay State. Scientists at the Massachusetts Institute of Technology and Harvard University played a key role in the explosion of the country's high-technology industries. Research laboratories and high-tech firms sprang up west of Boston and created thousands of well-paying jobs for Bay Staters. Although the economic recession of the early 1990s hit the area hard, a strong background in the high-tech and tourism industries helped Massachusetts recover.

Bostonians have had to face some of the worst traffic in the nation. In 1959, a highway known as the Central Artery was built to lessen the traffic. The highway ran right through the center of downtown Boston. When it was built, it comfortably carried about 75,000 vehicles a day. In a matter of years, that number increased to 200,000, and traffic was bumper-to-bumper for more than ten hours each day. The accident rate skyrocketed to four times the national average! Experts predicted that by 2010, the highway would be totally jammed for up to sixteen hours a day. Something had to be done.

Officials decided to replace the Central Artery with an underground expressway of eight to ten lanes. The plan, known as the Big Dig, outlined one of the most technically difficult and environmentally challenging infrastructure projects ever attempted in the United States. How could all of this be done without completely disrupting the city? It took a combination of project planners, environmental agencies, community groups, businesses, and politicians to come up with the solution.

Digging began in 1991. It was finally completed in 2006. Sixteen million cubic yards of dirt were excavated. It took 541,000 truckloads

The Big Dig, which took almost fifteen years to complete, inspired both praise and criticism.

to dump it all. Almost 4 million cubic yards of concrete were used—enough to make a sidewalk 3 feet wide and 4 inches thick from Boston to San Francisco and back three times. The Big Dig resulted in the creation of 300 acres of new parks. The enormous project had major glitches, however, including serious leaks and cost overruns. In 2006, the project became associated with tragedy when part of a tunnel's ceiling collapsed and a woman was killed while driving to Logan Airport. Some critics call the Big Dig one of the most mismanaged projects in American history.

Today, Massachusetts, in addition to having fewer traffic jams, remains a center of the high-tech industry in the eastern United States. It is also a leader in banking, education, insurance, and medical care. The state's future looks bright as the new century marches on.

Chapter Three

The Melting Pot

To most people from outside the United States, the word *Yankee* refers to any American. To those who live in the southern United States, a Yankee is a northerner. To New Englanders, to be a Yankee means to be a descendant of the original English settlers. Today, you can be a Yankee in Massachusetts no matter what your background—as long as you work hard, fight for what you believe in, and stay proud of your home state.

MAKING UP MASSACHUSETTS

Massachusetts is a crowded place, filled with people from all walks of life and every corner of the world. Although forty-five states are larger than Massachusetts, only twelve have a bigger population. About half the state's people live within 50 miles of Boston.

Yankees controlled Massachusetts for the first two hundred years of its history. By the mid-nineteenth century, however, a flood of new-comers began to challenge Yankee dominance. In the 1840s, hundreds of thousands of Irish men and women immigrated to Massachusetts

Its people's mix of cultural and ethnic backgrounds that helps make Massachusetts an enjoyable place to live.

POPULATION DENSITY

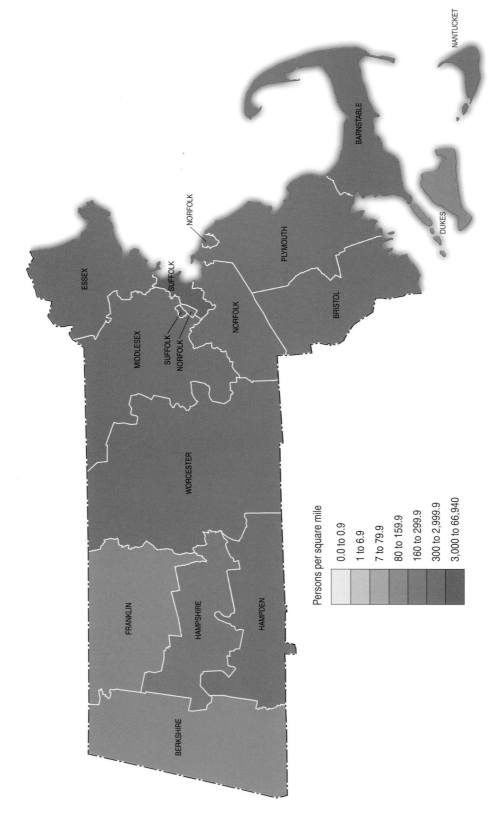

NANTUCKET

BARNSTABLE

NORFOLK

PLYMOUTH

ESSEX

SUFFOLK

DUKES

MIDDLESEX

SUFFOLK
NORFOLK

NORFOLK

BRISTOL

WORCESTER

Persons per square mile

0.0 to 0.9
1 to 6.9
7 to 79.9
80 to 159.9
160 to 299.9
300 to 2,999.9
3,000 to 66,940

FRANKLIN

HAMPSHIRE

HAMPDEN

BERKSHIRE

in search of work in the state's new industries. As manufacturing increased, so did the population. People arrived steadily from Canada, Scandinavia, and Germany. During the first half of the twentieth century, large numbers of Italians, Poles, Portuguese, Syrians, and Lebanese also moved to Massachusetts. After World War II, many African Americans left the southern states for Massachusetts in search of work and freedom.

Since the 1960s, the number of Puerto Ricans living in Massachusetts has risen dramatically. In Holyoke, more than 40 percent of the city's population is of Puerto Rican descent. Each year in July, the Latino community holds a Puerto Rican Day parade. It is one of the largest in the nation. According to 2005 figures, about 8 percent of the Bay State's population is Latino. In a fairly recent trend, many Latino immigrants are avoiding life in the bigger cities and instead heading to smaller towns such as Holyoke, Everett, Brockton, and Lawrence. The state's Latinos are battling a much higher than average poverty rate, and less than one-quarter are currently able to purchase a home.

In March 2006, thousands of immigration-reform supporters, many of them Latinos, demonstrate in downtown Boston.

A PORTUGUESE TRADITION IN NEW BEDFORD

For more than ninety years, New Bedford has celebrated the Feast of the Blessed Sacrament, an old Portuguese custom. The tradition comes from the island of Madeira, a Portuguese territory located 390 miles off the coast of Morocco.

In 1915, four Madeiran immigrants initiated the feast in New Bedford, a small city with a large Portuguese population. Until about 1945, the feast was mostly religious. It was marked by solemn Catholic masses as well as parades and picnics. Although the feast is still a holy tradition, it is also a chance for people of all backgrounds to explore the culture of Portugal and Portuguese Americans. Besides music and food, the celebration includes parades, amusement rides for children, and booths selling arts and crafts. The festival attracts about 300,000 people to New Bedford every year.

About one percent of Massachusetts citizens are Native Americans, most of whom live on Cape Cod and Martha's Vineyard. Members of the Abenaki, Algonquian, Apache, and Blackfoot groups still practice some of their traditions, including annual celebrations like the Planting Ceremony in the spring and the Harvest Ceremony in the fall, which honor the cycles of Earth, the Moon, the Sun, and the four seasons. Powwows are still held each year in Middleboro, Concord, and Westford. Some Massachusetts tribes still rely on a medicine man to lead ceremonies and to act as a spiritual advisor. A man named Cjegkitoonuppa (Slow Turtle), of the Wampanoag tribe, has helped the entire Native-American community for years. Traces of native culture can be found in the names of many towns and rivers of the region: Swampscott, Nantucket, Natick, the Narragansett River, Tumpum Pond—and the state's own name, Massachusetts.

African Americans make up about 7 percent of the Massachusetts population. The African-American community is largest in Boston, where one-fourth of the population is black. Despite its reputation of supporting civil rights, the city still suffers from racial tension. Integration has come a long way since the 1970s, however. African-American leaders abound in industry, academics, the arts, and politics throughout the state.

A group of African-American students takes a quick break in Boston.

Massachusetts also has a fast-growing Asian population. Throughout the state, the largest Asian cultural group is Chinese, followed by Indian, Vietnamese, and Cambodian. Boston's Chinatown section thrives with Chinese grocery stores, restaurants, and other businesses. The city of Lawrence has a substantial Vietnamese population. Many of these people are still struggling to fit into the larger community. "Maybe it would be easier for us if the economy was stronger," remarks a Vietnamese-born citizen. "I think that some people resent us because they think we're taking their jobs. But we just want to live and work and raise our children like they do."

ETHNIC MASSACHUSETTS

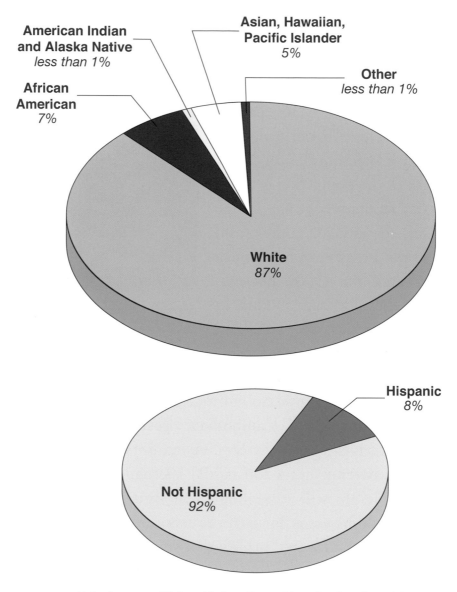

American Indian
and Alaska Native
less than 1%

Asian, Hawaiian,
Pacific Islander
5%

Other
less than 1%

African
American
7%

White
87%

Hispanic
8%

Not Hispanic
92%

*Note: A person of Cuban, Mexican, Puerto Rican, South or Central American,
or other Spanish culture or origin, regardless of race, is defined as Hispanic.*

Between 1990 and 2000, the Asian population of Massachusetts increased by more than 150 percent. Here, Cambodian-American brothers walk along the coastline.

Massachusetts becomes more diverse with each passing year. In recent years, an average of 23,000 people each year immigrated to Massachusetts from other countries. According to the Federation for American Immigration Reform (FAIR), the Bay State is the seventh most popular place for immigrants moving to the United States. According to FAIR, there were approximately 772,983 foreign-born people in the Massachusetts population in 2005. The majority of the state's recent newcomers are from China, the former Soviet republics, the Dominican Republic, and Haiti. Many others come from Brazil, Lebanon, and Southeast Asia. Recent immigrants have had a powerful effect on the state. Foreign-language newspapers have been created; ads and public-service announcements are being printed in several different languages; and ethnic grocery stores and restaurants have sprung up throughout the state. Schools have had to offer more and more English language learner (ELL) courses as well.

When traveling outside Massachusetts, many Bostonians are asked to say the sentence "Park the car in Harvard Yard." They are expected to say, "Pahk the cah in Havahd Yahd." There is more to the Boston accent than just dropping the letter *r*, however. Many native Bay Staters have more than an accent. They also have a vocabulary all their own. Here's a quick guide to understanding the local dialect.

Pronunciation: In Boston English, the *r* typically disappears when it is at the end of a word or when it precedes a consonant in the middle of a word: *vigor = vigah*; *weird = wee-id*; *corner = cawna*. Don't worry, the *r* doesn't totally "disappeah." Bostonians add it to the ends of words that end in an "ah" sound. In this case a word like *idea* sounds like "idear."

Vocabulary: Here are some terms unique to the Boston area, along with some words whose pronunciation is so unusual that non-natives may not even recognize them:

American chop suey: a popular lunch item made of macaroni, hamburger, and tomato sauce.

Bubbla: a water fountain.

Candlepin: a type of bowling with skinny pins and small balls.

 basement.

Cuber: the island called Cuba in the rest of the United States.

Foddy: the number after thirty-nine.

Tawnic: soda or pop.

The T: the subway.

Wicked: a general intensifier—i.e., wicked bad or wicked good.

Although religious freedom was the primary reason for the establishment of the Massachusetts colonies, the Puritans were anything but tolerant when it came to religion. In 1637, when a woman named Anne Hutchinson dared to question the basic principles of Puritanism, she was banished from the Massachusetts Bay Colony.

By the time of the Revolutionary War, other religions had begun to compete with Puritanism. Baptists and Methodists built churches in Boston, and the city's first Roman Catholic church was established in 1788. Mary Baker Eddy spread the Christian Scientist philosophy that the body could be healed through prayer when she founded the Church of Christ, Scientist, in Boston in 1879.

Today more than half of Massachusetts residents are Roman Catholic, making it the second most Catholic state in the country. The other half is mostly Protestant, with large groups of members of the United Church of Christ and the Episcopalian Church. A thriving Jewish community is prominent in the Boston area.

Many Chinese and Southeast Asian residents—foreign-born and U.S.-born alike—practice Buddhism. The Massachusetts Buddhist Association in Lexington has an active congregation from Taiwan and Hong Kong. A large Muslim community can be found in Sharon. In the 1900s, immigrants from Syria and Lebanon traveled to Massachusetts to work in Quincy's shipyards. Families began gathering together to worship, and in 1934, they formed the Arab American Banner Society. Almost thirty years later, the community built a mosque in Sharon. Imam Talal Eid, who moved to Massachusetts to lead the mosque in the early 1980s, says, "Being an imam in America is totally different from being an imam in Lebanon. There my role was limited to the mosque and dealing with the community, but here it is a combination: I lead the prayer, do the education, do the counseling and deal with people of different backgrounds, cultures, nationalities and languages. The Islamic Center of New England is a small replica of the United Nations, with more than 25 different nationalities."

A NEW DIRECTION IN EDUCATION

Massachusetts citizens take the education of their children very seriously. The state's educators are known for their openness to trying new approaches. For example, in 2005, educational reformers started the Expanding Learning Time to Support Student Success Initiative. The initiative's goal is simple: in order for children to learn everything that the state and the nation expect them to learn, they need more time. According to the initiative's philosophy, the average school day or year has to be 30 percent longer.

Ten Massachusetts schools were selected to begin the Expanding Learning Time program in the 2006–2007 school year. Initiative leaders are keeping a close eye on how well the strategy works. If the results are promising, more schools will start trying the program. In this way, a simple initiative would transform the way education happens across the state. Even if the initiative doesn't work, it is an example of people's openness to challenging long-standing traditions.

CELEBRATIONS

There's almost always a celebration or festival going on in Massachusetts. Wintertime festivities include Boston's First Night celebration on New Year's Eve (complete with ice sculptures and fireworks), the Winter Carnival in Northampton, and the Boston Common Christmas Festival. In the fall, the town of Plymouth re-creates Thanksgiving, the Head of the Charles Regatta features rowing races on the Charles River, and Harwich holds the Cranberry Harvest Festival. Summertime is marked by the playful Sandcastle Contest on Nantucket Island and the Fishermen's Memorial Service in Gloucester.

The Bay State also proudly commemorates important dates in its history. Evacuation Day, the day the British left Massachusetts, is marked by parades in South Boston on March 17. On the third Monday of April, Patriot's Day—the beginning of the American Revolution—is observed in Lexington, Concord, and many other towns with reenactments and parades. On June 17, the Battle of Bunker Hill is commemorated with a ceremony in Charlestown.

The Battle of Lexington is reenacted at Lexington Green Park each year on Patriot's Day.

On warm summer nights, many Bostonians stretch out on the grassy banks of the Charles River to listen to the Boston Pops Orchestra perform at a stage called the Hatch Shell. For years the Boston Pops have charmed audiences with orchestral versions of popular songs by Irving Berlin, Rogers and Hammerstein, and even the Beatles. Free concerts and movie screenings are held at the Hatch Shell all summer long. "I live at the Hatch Shell in the summer," says Emerson College student Maria Ameche. "Even as a poor student, I can hear classical music, see my favorite pop bands, and watch movies at sunset without a dollar in my pocket."

The last thing you want to do in Massachusetts is insult the local sports teams. Indeed, there's no faster way to inflame the fiery New England temper. Bay State sports fans love their teams with a passion.

Take, for example, the Red Sox. For eighty-six years, starting in 1918, the Sox could not get their hands on a World Series win. Despite what seemed like a curse, fans remained staunchly loyal to the team that has fielded a parade of baseball superstars like Carl Yastrzemski and Jim Rice.

In 2004, the curse was broken. The Sox came back from a 3–0 deficit to beat the Yankees in the American League Division Series (ALDS), then defeated the St. Louis Cardinals to win the World Series. It was an incredible moment to be from Massachusetts. People throughout the state poured into the streets to celebrate after the final out. Red Sox owner John Henry said, "This is sheer relief and joy for all New England." General manager Theo Epstein said, "This is what we've all been waiting for. We can die happy. I just hope everyone out there who has been rooting for the Red Sox for the last 86 years is enjoying this as much as we are." In 2007, the Sox did it again. They came back from a 3–1 deficit in the ALDS and then swept the Colorado Rockies to win the World Series.

Massachusetts rejoices when the Red Sox win the World Series in 2007. Most Valuable Player Mike Lowell's grin is almost as big as his trophy.

The New England Patriots have been around since 1959 and are a familiar team at recent Super Bowls. They lost to the Chicago Bears in 1986, the Green Bay Packers in 1997, and the New York Giants in 2008, but took the Super Bowl championship from the St. Louis Rams in 2002, the Carolina Panthers in 2004, and the Philadelphia Eagles in 2005.

Since basketball was invented in Springfield, Massachusetts, in 1891, Boston has been known for its success on the court. With such great players as Larry Bird and Bill Russell, the Boston Celtics have won sixteen National Basketball Association championships. Coach Arnold "Red" Auerback once said, "The Celtics aren't a team. They're a way of life."

New England Patriots quarterback Tom Brady celebrates a Super Bowl XXXIX win over the Philadelphia Eagles on February 6, 2005.

Massachusetts athletes succeed on the ice as well. The Boston Bruins hockey team has produced such superstars as Bobby Orr and Ray Bourque.

The varied terrain of Massachusetts provides Bay Staters with many opportunities to enjoy outdoor sports. Trout fishing is particularly good in the Berkshires, while saltwater fishing for striped bass, bluefish, and giant tuna off the Atlantic coast is a favorite New England pastime. Hunters flock to Massachusetts for the deer, pheasant, and grouse seasons. In winter, Massachusetts offers plenty of skiing and snowboarding, and when the local lakes and ponds freeze over, it's time to lace up the ice skates. Many residents and tourists spend summers swimming, sunbathing, and feasting on lobster at Cape Cod beaches. Crisp fall days are perfect for apple picking and taking in the colorful foliage in western Massachusetts.

Spring brings the nation's oldest and most famous footrace, the Boston Marathon. First run in 1897, the annual race draws thousands of runners and hundreds of thousands of fans from all over the world. The grueling 26-mile run begins in the suburb of Hopkinton and ends in Boston's Back Bay. "I placed twenty-sixth . . . when I ran the Boston Marathon," Dan Fusilier recalls. "And even though I didn't win, I count finishing that race as one of my fondest memories. The city was beautiful, and the fans lining the streets and clapping made all the runners feel great."

Runners take off at the beginning of the 111th Boston Marathon in April 2007.

Chapter Four

Massachusetts for the People

The Massachusetts Constitution was written by John Adams and adopted during the American Revolution in 1780, seven years before the U.S. Constitution was finished. It is the oldest working constitution in the world. Massachusetts is the only one of the first thirteen states to be ruled by its original document. The state's political life remains about as vital as it was back in the early days of the Union. "Growing up, all I heard about in my house was politics. It was everyone's pastime," says Rita Moan, a lifelong Massachusetts resident. "Learning about how the government really worked—or was supposed to work—made listening to the political arguments all the more fun."

INSIDE GOVERNMENT

The Massachusetts Constitution divides the state's government into three branches: executive, judicial, and legislative.

The Massachusetts State House in Boston was built on a pasture owned by John Hancock.

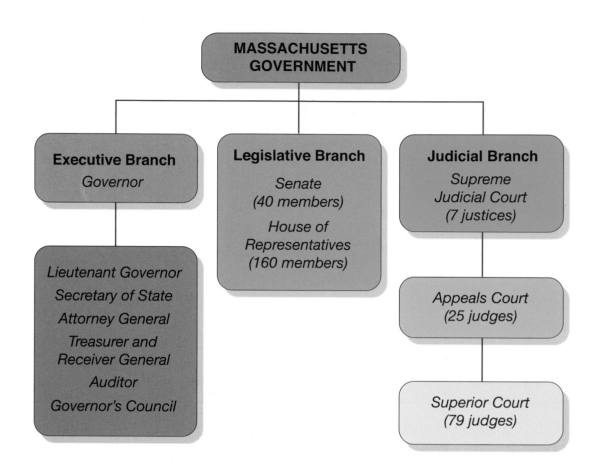

MASSACHUSETTS GOVERNMENT

Executive Branch
Governor

Lieutenant Governor
Secretary of State
Attorney General
Treasurer and Receiver General
Auditor
Governor's Council

Legislative Branch
Senate (40 members)
House of Representatives (160 members)

Judicial Branch
Supreme Judicial Court (7 justices)
Appeals Court (25 judges)
Superior Court (79 judges)

Executive Branch

The head of the executive branch is the governor, who serves a four-year term. He or she appoints department heads and judges and prepares a budget for submission to the legislature. The governor also holds the power of veto, which means he or she can reject a law passed by the legislature.

A lieutenant governor, attorney general, secretary of state, treasurer, auditor, and governor's council also are elected for four-year terms. The governor's council, which includes the lieutenant governor and eight people elected by region, reviews the governor's judicial appointments.

Legislative Branch

The Massachusetts legislature, known as the General Court, consists of a 40-member senate and a 160-member house of representatives. Legislators are elected to two-year terms. The General Court votes on bills proposed by its members or by regular citizens. The Bay State's legislative process is unique in that any citizen can submit a bill to the legislature. A public hearing is held for every proposed bill. Two-thirds of the members of both houses must vote yes to pass a bill or to overturn the governor's veto.

Judicial Branch

The supreme judicial court is the highest court in Massachusetts. Established in 1692, it is the nation's oldest continuously operating court. It consists of a chief justice and six associate justices. Oliver Wendell Holmes, who led the state's supreme court from 1899 to 1902 and later served on the U.S. Supreme Court, was one of the nation's greatest judicial minds. Known for his commitment to social justice, Holmes once wrote, "Beware how you take away hope from any human being."

The appeals court, with twenty-five judges, is the state's second-highest court. If someone disagrees with a decision in a superior court—the state's main trial court—he or she can ask the appeals court to review it. Judges are appointed by the governor, but the governor's council must agree to the appointments. Judges may serve until they reach seventy years of age.

Oliver Wendell Holmes discouraged fellow Supreme Court judges from letting their personal opinions affect their decisions.

TAXACHUSETTS

Income taxes provide approximately 75 percent of the income of Massachusetts. The state also collects property taxes, motor fuel taxes, and sales taxes. During the 1970s, taxes in Massachusetts soared so high that the state earned the nickname Taxachusetts. Since then, voters passed Proposition 2 1/2, which cut property taxes dramatically. "No one likes to pay taxes, and neither do I," says one Worcester resident. "And I think we could be smarter about where we spend our money—our schools need more help, for one thing, and so many people are without health insurance. But then you look at what does work in the state and how much we've got to be proud of, and you figure it's worth it."

Today, the state's taxes are much lower than they once were. The trend to cut taxes will likely continue. Perhaps in the near future, the nickname Taxachusetts will be laid to rest once and for all.

BAY STATE POLITICS

Throughout the early nineteenth century, Massachusetts voters generally supported the Federalist Party and, later, the Republican Party. Then immigration changed the face of politics, as people of all backgrounds demanded representation. Newcomers tended to vote Democratic. In 1914, Democrat David I. Walsh became the state's first Catholic governor. During the 1950s, the Democratic Party took hold of the Massachusetts legislature, and it has held its grip ever since. As was true in much of the country, the state became more conservative in the 1980s and 1990s. Recent Republican governors William F. Weld, Paul Cellucci, and Mitt Romney concentrated on lowering taxes and minimizing the size of the state government.

In 2006, Deval Patrick was elected governor of the Bay State. He moved to Massachusetts when he was fourteen years old and had a scholarship to

Elected in 2006, Deval Patrick is the first African-American governor of Massachusetts.

Milton Academy, an independent school south of Boston. He went on to Harvard University and then spent a year working with the United Nations in the Darfur region of Sudan in Africa. After getting his law degree, Patrick worked as a lawyer until former president Bill Clinton appointed him assistant attorney general for civil rights in the U.S. Department of Justice. In this position, Patrick led a major criminal investigation into a series of church burnings throughout the South.

Patrick is the first African-American governor of Massachusetts. Since he was elected, he and his family have lived in Milton. Their house happens to be one that Patrick served on his paper route when he was in high school.

One of the familiar faces on the presidential docket in 2007 was former Massachusetts governor Mitt Romney. Elected as governor in 2002, he helped the state turn its economy around.

THE KENNEDY LEGACY

No name looms as large in Massachusetts politics as Kennedy. Wealthy, highly educated, and handsome, this powerful Brookline family was headed by Joseph Patrick Kennedy, an Irish-Catholic entrepreneur and diplomat who sent his four sons to Harvard University and instilled in them a sense of duty to public service. The eldest son, Joseph Jr., was killed during World War II. The other three sons—John, Robert, and Edward—served the state and the nation as political leaders.

While representing Massachusetts in the U.S. Senate, John F. Kennedy was elected president. His assassination in 1963 shocked the nation. In 1968, John's brother Robert also was serving as a U.S. senator—and campaigning for the Democratic presidential nomination—when he was assassinated. The youngest son, Edward, is still a member of the U.S. Senate today. Although plagued by scandal and turmoil, the

This Kennedy family portrait was taken in 1934. From left to right, it shows Edward, Jeanne, Robert, Patricia, Eunice, Kathleen, Rosemary, John, Mrs. Rose Kennedy, and Joseph P. Kennedy.

Kennedy family legacy remains strong. "There was a future there," jewelry store clerk Wesley Cwieka of Chicopee recalls. "They did good for the people."

DEALING WITH CONTROVERSY

Massachusetts lawmakers have a history of tackling important but sensitive issues. For example, Massachusetts was the first state to legalize same-sex marriages. This was a highly controversial move.

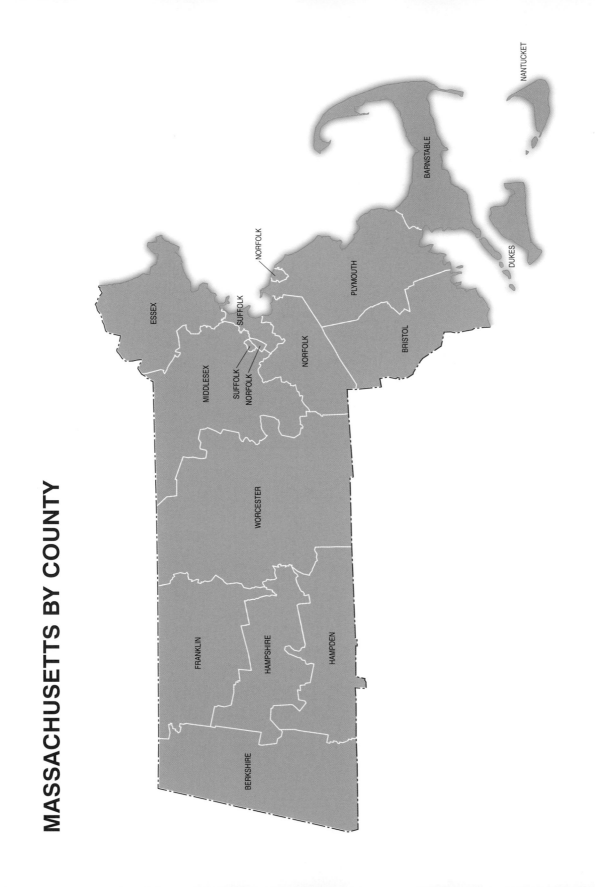

MASSACHUSETTS BY COUNTY

NANTUCKET

BARNSTABLE

DUKES

NORFOLK

PLYMOUTH

ESSEX

SUFFOLK

BRISTOL

MIDDLESEX

NORFOLK

SUFFOLK

NORFOLK

WORCESTER

FRANKLIN

HAMPSHIRE

HAMPDEN

BERKSHIRE

In April 2006, the Massachusetts legislature approved a bill that requires all residents to purchase health insurance, or else face legal punishment. Former Massachusetts governor Mitt Romney said, "We insist that everybody who drives a car has insurance, and cars are a lot less expensive than people." No other U.S. state has tried this approach to the problem of inadequate health coverage for so many people. "Massachusetts is the first state in America to reach full adulthood," claimed Uwe Reinhart, a professor of economics at Princeton University.

Another law being considered by the Massachusetts legislature would prohibit Massachusetts drivers from smoking inside a vehicle while in the presence of a child who is under the age of five or weighs less than 40 pounds. First-time offenders would be fined $25, and repeat offenders would be fined $100. Some people argue that this law would trample on the rights of smokers and parents, while others believe that secondhand smoke inside cars severely threatens children's health. Massachusetts legislators continue to take on new and different issues and often inspire other states to follow their lead.

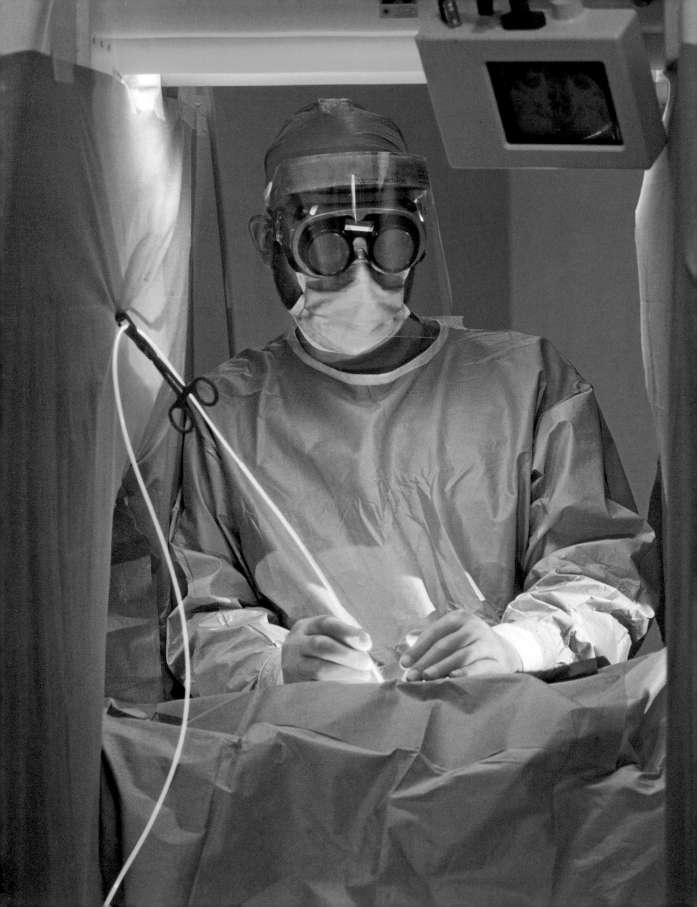

Chapter Five

Made in Massachusetts

New Englanders have long been known for their strong work ethic. Ralph Waldo Emerson, one of the nation's great literary figures, captured this spirit when he wrote, "The reward of a thing well done is to have done it." Early Bay Staters used a bit of Yankee ingenuity and lots of hard work to turn their one-man shops into the nation's first textile factories. The modern textile industry began in Waltham in 1814, when the Boston Manufacturing Company began processing raw cotton and weaving it into finished cloth all under one roof. Later, the shoemaking industry also boomed throughout the state. Paper manufacturers began putting the textile mills' waste to use in making fine grades of paper. These manufacturers, along with rubber producers, became the basis of the state's industry until World War II.

Between 1988 and 1991, the Massachusetts economy took a serious dip as the entire nation suffered a recession. Employment in construction dropped 44 percent, real-estate jobs went down almost 24 percent, unemployment reached 9 percent, and more than 100,000 wholesale and retail trade jobs were lost. It took until the late 1990s for the economy to rebound.

The Massachusetts economy increasingly relies on high-tech and service industries. Here, a doctor uses specialized magnets to treat a patient.

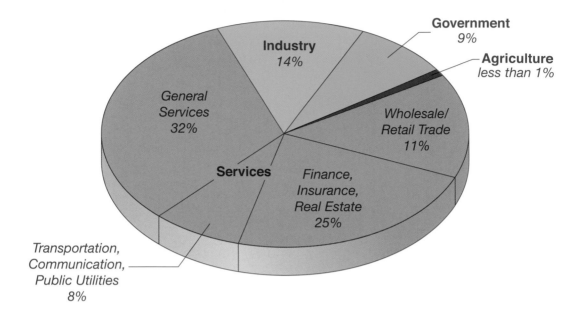

2006 GROSS STATE PRODUCT: $337.6 Million

- Government 9%
- Agriculture less than 1%
- Wholesale/Retail Trade 11%
- Finance, Insurance, Real Estate 25%
- Transportation, Communication, Public Utilities 8%
- Services
- General Services 32%
- Industry 14%

The explosion in information technology helped speed things up. In late 2005, the Bay State's economy finally began growing at a steady rate, and more than 57,000 jobs were added to the market. Tourism increased, especially in Boston, and exports hit an all-time high. Since then, Massachusetts has had strong indications of a reliable and powerful economy.

Today, manufacturing accounts for about one-fifth of the Massachusetts economy. The state's largest area of manufacturing is machinery, particularly computers and other electronic products. Massachusetts companies began making personal home computers in the early 1970s. Today, the state contains the largest area of high-tech manufacturing east of the Mississippi River. A host of electrical products, from home appliances to electronic components for aerospace engineering, also are produced in the state.

In 1638, the first printing press in the English colonies was set up in Cambridge, Massachusetts. Since then, Boston has become a major printing and publishing center. The state publishes more than 300 newspapers and about 450 magazines. Massachusetts factories manufacture boxes, paper goods, and greeting cards. Other major industries include the manufacture of precision instruments, transportation equipment, fabricated metals for guns, knives and tools, plastic goods, wool carpets, processed foods, and chemicals for photography development and cleaning products.

At the Woods Hole Oceanographic Institute, a worker stands next to a fleet of thermal gliders. Scientists use instruments inside the gliders to understand how oceans affect climate change.

Massachusetts is one of the nation's leaders in commercial fishing. When early explorers like John Cabot and Bartholomew Gosnold sailed Massachusetts Bay, they caught so much cod that they couldn't transport it all, and they threw most of it back. At one time, New Bedford fishermen provided almost 90 percent of the scallops sold in the United States. Those numbers have dropped continually, but scallop fishing is still an important industry. Gloucester companies catch immense quantities of flounder, haddock, ocean perch, and whiting.

The state's fishing industry is growing smaller every year, however, partly because fishing companies are finding it more expensive to operate their fleets. In addition, overfishing has so severely depleted stocks of flounder and other fish that Massachusetts restaurant owners now depend on suppliers in Iceland and Norway for much of their fish. "My grandfather fished; so did my father. In fact, when I was growing up, I barely knew anybody who *didn't* make a living on the water," remarks a third-generation fisherman from New Bedford. "But I don't know how long I'll be able to manage to hang on. It gets tougher every year. A whole way of life seems to be dying right before my eyes. I guess I'll have to learn to do something else. I'm sure teaching my kids about other options."

Scallop fishermen empty their catch near Fairhaven. This boat is part of an aquaculture company that farms scallops in Nasketucket Bay.

TOUGH TIMES ON THE SEA

Sometimes technology can bring as much harm to an industry as good. This is true when it comes to New England fisheries. In the late 1960s, the U.S. fishing industry began to fall behind as other countries started fishing U.S. waters with huge, technologically advanced ships. These floating factories could catch thousands more fish than their small, old-fashioned American counterparts.

U.S. government officials responded by banning foreign fleets from American waters. They also sank funds into developing high-tech equipment like Loran-C, a sonar system that enables fishermen to track schools of fish. Thanks to such innovations, in the late 1980s the Massachusetts fishing industry had its largest catch since 1945.

Here's the real catch: the very technology that allows Massachusetts fishing companies to survive tough competition is slowly killing the industry altogether. With high-tech help, fishermen have gotten too good at their trade. As fish become scarcer, the industry has responded by creating even better technology to capture the now harder-to-find fish.

The situation has left the fish population of New England severely depleted. Since 1990, the average New England catch has dropped 30 percent. The numbers of halibut and haddock, two Massachusetts staples, have dropped dangerously low. This may be the price paid for what seems to be a case of overly effective technology. As Massachusetts fishing industry leader Vito J. Calomo remarked in 1996, "Man-with-technology versus fish is a whole other thing than man versus fish."

Farming is a small but important part of the state's economy. Massachusetts is the second-largest producer of cranberries in the nation. According to Native-American mythology, a dove carried the first cranberry from heaven to Earth in its beak. The cranberry has proven heaven-sent for the state economy for more than two centuries. Many of the nation's flowers and shrubs come from Massachusetts nurseries and greenhouses. The state is also a producer of milk, maple syrup, sweet corn, and apples.

A young man harvests cranberries on Nantucket Island.

EARNING A LIVING

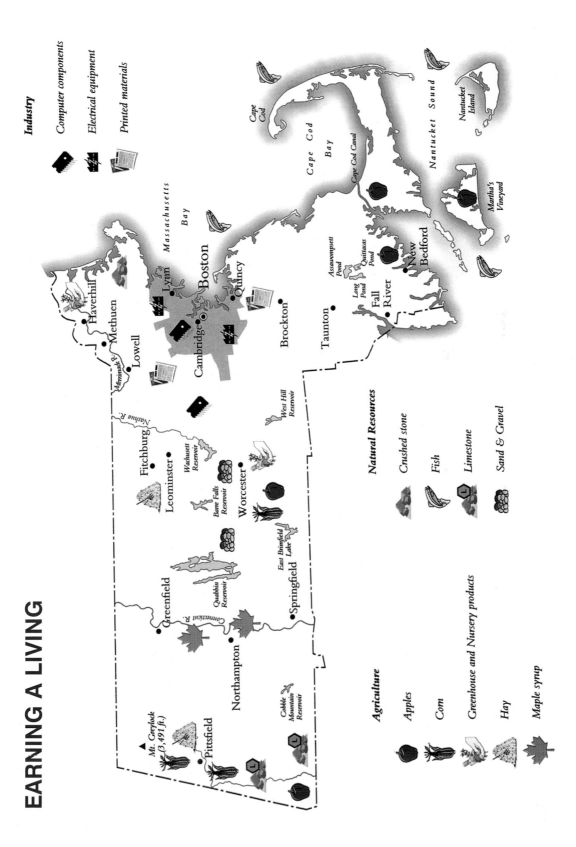

Industry

- Computer components
- Electrical equipment
- Printed materials

Natural Resources

- Crushed stone
- Fish
- Limestone
- Sand & Gravel

Agriculture

- Apples
- Corn
- Greenhouse and Nursery products
- Hay
- Maple syrup

SERVING THE BAY STATE

The largest segment of the state's economy is service industries, in which workers provide services to other people instead of making a product. Profitable service industries include health care, private education, law, computer-programming services, and engineering. The computer software industry is among the fastest-growing sectors of the Massachusetts economy. Finance, real estate, and banking are also important service industries. Boston is known as a leading center of medical research.

Tourism is a huge service industry in Massachusetts. Approximately 26 million tourists visit Massachusetts each year. They typically bring in $11 billion annually while visiting Boston, Plymouth, and Salem's historic sights and relaxing on Nantucket Island, Martha's Vineyard, and the beaches of Cape Cod and Cape Ann.

AN EDUCATION POWERHOUSE

Education is a major source of employment for Massachusetts residents. About one million students attend more than 1,800 elementary and secondary schools. More than a hundred colleges and universities have earned Massachusetts a reputation as one of the finest places to learn in the world.

The Bay State has a long history as a pioneer in education. The first public secondary school in the colonies, Boston Latin, was founded in 1635. The following year, Harvard became the colonies' first college, and in 1821 the English High School became the first public high school in the nation. As early as 1642, citizens enacted laws requiring the teaching of reading and writing. By 1647, every town of fifty or more people had to establish a school funded by taxes. In 1852, Massachusetts became the first state to declare school attendance mandatory, and two years later, the free textbook law went into effect. All children, rich or poor, would be educated.

Today, more than twenty colleges and universities flourish in the Boston area alone. These highly regarded schools include Tufts, Brandeis, Wellesley, Boston University, Boston College, College of the Holy Cross, and Northeastern University, the nation's largest private university. In Cambridge, the Massachusetts Institute of Technology is a world-famous center of scientific research, and Harvard University is the oldest and best-known university in the United States. Among Harvard's graduates are seven U.S. presidents and more than forty Nobel Prize winners. Some of the most talented young musicians in the country are drawn to the New England Conservatory, the Boston Conservatory, and the Berklee College of Music.

Prestigious colleges and universities lie outside the Boston area as well. Amherst College is one of the nation's top-rated liberal arts colleges, and the women's colleges of Mount Holyoke in South Hadley and Smith in

Happy scholars graduate from Harvard Business School.

Northampton are excellent. Students from many places in the world attend Williams College, where they can learn about the universe at the oldest astronomical observatory in the country. With its five campuses located in Amherst, Boston, Dartmouth, Lowell, and Worcester, the University of Massachusetts has graduated students who went on to become Pulitzer Prize winners, American Book Award winners, and Nobel Laureates.

The concentration of so many distinguished universities in Massachusetts boosts the state's economy. Research conducted by professors at these universities has led to the development of many scientific and medical innovations. This concentration of talent attracts even more professionals and intellectuals from around the world.

MASSACHUSETTS WORKFORCE

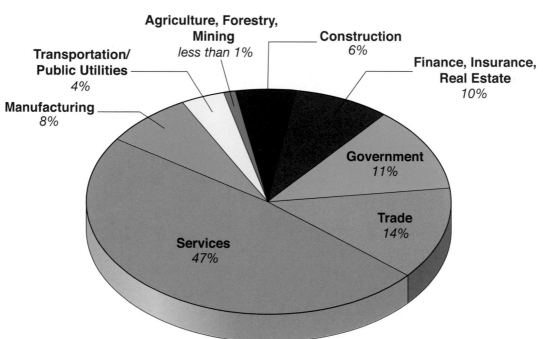

Agriculture, Forestry, Mining
less than 1%

Construction
6%

Transportation/
Public Utilities
4%

Finance, Insurance,
Real Estate
10%

Manufacturing
8%

Government
11%

Trade
14%

Services
47%

In the last few years, the Massachusetts economy has improved; this can be seen in its growth in exports. In the first six months of 2004, income from exports was at $11 billion, which was a 23-percent increase from the same period in 2003. Nationwide, exports increased only 14 percent during the same time span. Pharmaceutical products were up 93 percent, while medical devices and instruments were up 35 percent. "Within the U.S., we have very competitive industries compared to other states," says Andre Mayer, senior vice president for research at Associated Industries of Massachusetts.

Massachusetts plays a major role in the growing global economy. It exports thousands of products throughout the world. Top exports include electric machinery, plastics, pearls and precious stones, paper and printed materials, toys and games, iron and steel, aircraft parts, clothing, rubber, cosmetics, glass, musical instruments, and many more goods.

At the Hasbro manufacturing facility in East Longmeadow—the nation's largest domestic game-production facility—Darth Vader and two Stormtroopers supervise production.

Chapter Six

Bay State Road Trip

A trip through Massachusetts is like a trip through time. Preserved land-marks and tributes to an earlier time serve as vivid reminders of the state's fascinating history. This state has a landscape as rich as its history—rugged mountains, fertile valleys, bustling cities, haunted villages, rocky shorelines, and sandy beaches. Massachusetts is brimming with beauty and tradition.

THE BERKSHIRES

The westernmost part of Massachusetts is the state's most mountainous region. In the Berkshires, opportunities abound for rock climbing, hiking, fishing, biking, and canoeing. Snowy mountain resorts like Cranwell Resort in Lenox and Wachusett in Princeton lure skiers in the winter. In the summer, thousands of people flock to the Tanglewood Music Festival in Lenox and to dance and theater festivals in Lee, Williamstown, and Stockbridge. "Some of the most enjoyable and stimulating opportunities I've had as an actor have been at the Williamstown Theater Festival," says James Judy, a New York actor who has performed on Broadway.

An actor impersonating Benjamin Franklin greets visitors on the Boston Freedom Trail.

The fall foliage is gorgeous along the Mohawk Trail between Greenfield and Williamstown. Some people say it offers New England foliage at its finest. Today the trail follows 63 miles of modern highway, but three hundred years ago, it was a footpath carved out by the Pocomtuc Native Americans. Later, pioneers used the trail to reach the Mohawk and Hudson valleys in present-day New York. Along the trail are dozens of historical markers commemorating Native-American battles and the migration of early European pioneers.

This monument on the Mohawk Trail is dedicated to the Five Indian Nations of the Mohawk Sunrise.

PLACES TO SEE

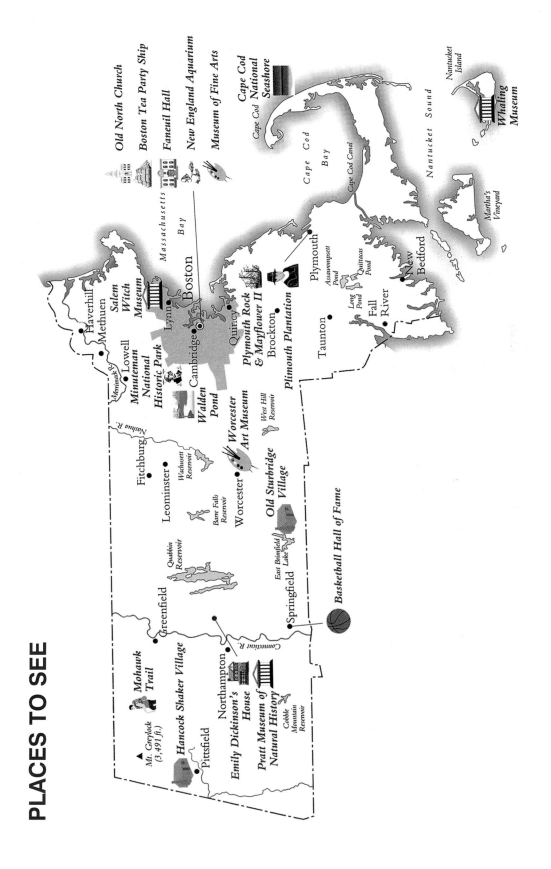

Old North Church

Boston Tea Party Ship

Faneuil Hall

New England Aquarium

Museum of Fine Arts

Cape Cod National Seashore

Whaling Museum

Nantucket Island

Nantucket Sound

Cape Cod

Cape Cod Bay

Cape Cod Canal

Martha's Vineyard

Massachusetts Bay

New Bedford

Plymouth

Assawompsett Pond

Quittacas Pond

Long Pond

Fall River

Taunton

Salem Witch Museum

Boston

Lynn

Cambridge

Quincy

Plymouth Rock & Mayflower II

Brockton

Plimouth Plantation

Haverhill

Methuen

Lowell

Minuteman National Historic Park

Walden Pond

Worcester Art Museum

West Hill Reservoir

Merrimack R.

Nashua R.

Fitchburg

Leominster

Wachusett Reservoir

Barre Falls Reservoir

Worcester

Old Sturbridge Village

East Brimfield Lake

Basketball Hall of Fame

Quabbin Reservoir

Greenfield

Springfield

Connecticut R.

Mohawk Trail

Mt. Greylock (3,491 ft.)

Hancock Shaker Village

Pittsfield

Emily Dickinson's House

Northampton

Pratt Museum of Natural History

Cobble Mountain Reservoir

In the Connecticut River valley town of Amherst, you'll find the lifelong residence of Emily Dickinson. Touring her house, you can see the room where she wrote most of her poems. The Amherst College Museum of Natural History houses a fine collection of ancient skeletons, meteorites, and Native-American artifacts.

Worcester, the state's second-largest city, is home to the Worcester Art Museum, one of the nation's best. Here you can see everything from ancient Egyptian artifacts to paintings by the French master Claude Monet. The American Antiquarian Society holds some of the world's oldest newspapers.

At the Dickinson Homestead in Amherst, Emily wrote poems that are still read in schools today.

AND THEN THERE WAS LIGHT: SPOTLIGHT ON GREAT BARRINGTON

You might not find the name of Great Barrington in most American history books, but this little town in western Massachusetts has a fascinating past. In 1774, the town hosted one of the earliest acts of open resistance to the British. This act symbolically lit the fuse of the American Revolution. That year, 1,500 men gathered around the Great Barrington Courthouse and demanded the end of British rule. Although no shots were fired during their protest, it was a revolutionary moment—they succeeded in driving the British magistrates out of the courthouse. This helped begin a chain reaction that eventually led to American independence.

Great Barrington's tradition of freedom continued as its residents supported the antislavery movement. In 1783, the town hosted a trial in which a slave named Elizabeth Freeman won her freedom. This was the first case that established slavery as unconstitutional in Massachusetts. Eighty-five years later, the town produced another crucial player in African-American history, W. E. B. Du Bois. Du Bois became a prolific and powerful civil rights activist and leader in the National Association for the Advancement of Colored People.

One of the town's "brightest" moments came in 1886, when Great Barrington became the first town in the United States to be lit by electric streetlights. After townsman William Stanley invented the first electrical transformer, he ran electrical wires along Main Street and connected them to local businesses. He threw the switch, and light shone upon the town.

A little southwest of Worcester, visitors journey back to a simpler time by visiting Old Sturbridge Village, a re-creation of an 1830s New England village. It features forty restored structures, including a school, a tavern, a bank, shops, churches, and homes, as well as a working farm and a water-powered mill. The staff wears historically accurate costumes. "I used to take my kids here so they could see what life was like before television and cars," says Ron Parker, a grandfather of four. "But now that they're grown and moved away, I come here about once a year by myself, just for the quiet and simplicity of it all. I can't wait to take my grandkids here."

A visit to Old Sturbridge Village is like stepping back in time. Here, workers show what it was like to build a barn almost two centuries ago.

The state's third-largest city, Springfield, is the sight of the nation's first federal armory. The Springfield Armory National Historic Site displays many weapons that were first developed there. Springfield is also the birthplace of basketball. Sports fans can visit the Basketball Hall of Fame to learn about the history of the sport and its greatest players.

Almost a century ago, Massachusetts officials worried that the fast-growing city of Boston would run out of water. They looked for a place to build an additional reservoir and decided that the Swift River valley would be perfectly suited. The valley is fed by three branches of the Swift River.

At the Basketball Hall of Fame in Springfield, elite players are displayed on the Honors Ring.

Putting in one simple dam would create an enormous lake. No landmarks or highways were in the way, but there were four small towns. The towns' 2,500 inhabitants had to move, and more than a thousand homes, barns, churches, schools, and stores were knocked down. More than 7,600 graves also had to be dug up and moved.

In 1926, the huge engineering project began. Construction continued for twenty years, and in 1946, officials declared the Quabbin Reservoir full. Today, the Quabbin is the largest man-made reservoir in the world. It is also the main source of drinking water for forty-six Boston-area communities. People also use the reservoir for boating and fishing.

The Quabbin Reservoir is a source of leisure activities as well as drinking water.

LEXINGTON AND CONCORD

Heading toward Boston, you'll first pass through the history-laden towns of Lexington and Concord, where the American Revolution began in 1775. In Lexington, visitors retrace the steps of the Revolution's first skirmish at the Lexington Battle Green, visit the Old Belfry that summoned the militia to the green, and have their pictures taken in front of the Revolutionary Monument, which was built in 1799. Down the street, the National Heritage Museum has exhibits of costumes, furniture, and toys from the Revolutionary period.

In neighboring Concord, a must-see is the Minute Man National Historical Park. Here you can follow the steps of the British soldiers as they marched into town on April 19, 1775. The fight that erupted launched the

This reproduction of Old North Bridge helps visitors imagine what it must have been like when the minutemen fought the British in Concord on April 19, 1775.

American Revolution. Concord was also once home to some of the nation's leading literary figures. Visitors can tour the homes of Ralph Waldo Emerson and Nathaniel Hawthorne as well as Orchard House, the residence of Louisa May Alcott and the setting for her novel *Little Women*. After taking in all this history, visitors can gather their thoughts and find a bit of serenity in the wooded trails of Walden Pond, just as writer Henry David Thoreau did in the nineteenth century. Thoreau's final resting place—along with those of Emerson, Alcott, and Hawthorne—is in the nearby Sleepy Hollow Cemetery.

Concord's Walden Pond looks as peaceful today as it did when Thoreau built a cabin near its shores.

THE NORTH SHORE

The North Shore stretches from Boston to Cape Ann. Cape Ann is home to the picturesque towns of Gloucester and Rockport. Gloucester is a town that still lives off the sea. It is the site of the famous fisherman statue—perhaps better known as the Gorton's Fisherman, because the seafood company uses it on all its packaging—which was built as a tribute to all the fishermen who have given their lives at sea.

Visitors to the North Shore often take a break to enjoy a seafood lunch of the freshest catch in New England before they experience some of the area's cultural attractions. Art lovers head to Rockport, a seaside town chock-full of artists. The James Babson Cooperage Shop, on the outskirts of town, displays early American tools and furniture. The Rockport Art Association

The waters of Rockport are often filled with lobster boats.

shows the work of local artists. Cape Ann is also an excellent place to join a whale-watching tour, during which people are almost guaranteed to spot a whale in its natural habitat.

Moving south from Cape Ann, you might want to stop by the beautiful town of Marblehead to see some well-kept nineteenth-century mansions. Also be sure to reach Salem, the site of the infamous witch trials of 1692. The Salem Witch Museum gives visitors a look at one of the most emotional and tragic events of early American history. The town draws more than a million tourists each year. They enjoy getting spooked at the Salem Witch Village, the Witch House, and the Witch Dungeon Museum, which features a re-creation of a witch trial adapted from actual court transcripts.

At the Salem Witch Museum, visitors explore a dark period in American history.

BOSTON

Boston, the state's capital and largest city, is itself worth a trip to Massachusetts. It is a historic city, a modern metropolis, and a cultural center all in one. There is much to see and even more to do.

Historic Boston

The Boston Public Garden, located smack-dab in the middle of the city, is a good place to begin a tour. Walkers and bikers fill the paths that cut through the flower-filled garden. The lawns are covered with professionals taking lunch breaks, people walking their dogs, and students. Children take rides on the famous swan boats and play on the iron ducklings that are a tribute to the classic children's story *Make Way for Ducklings* by Robert McCloskey.

People fill the lawns and swan boats of the Boston Public Garden on a sunny spring day.

The Public Garden leads to the Boston Common, the country's oldest public park and the beginning of the Freedom Trail, a 2.5-mile walking tour that links sixteen of Boston's most important historic landmarks. Among these landmarks are the Park Street Church, where William Lloyd Garrison gave his first antislavery speech; the Old South Meeting House, where the Boston Tea Party was planned; the Paul Revere House; and the Old North Church, where lanterns were hung to warn the colonists of British invasion.

Also along the Freedom Trail is one of the city's most popular tourist attractions, Faneuil Hall. Once the meeting place and market where the patriots of the American Revolution gathered, Faneuil Hall is next to the more modern Quincy Market, which includes more than 125 restaurants and shops. The Freedom Trail ends at Bunker Hill, where a monument commemorates the 1775 Revolutionary War battle.

The lights, sounds, shops, and excitement of Faneuil Hall and Quincy Market attract tourists to the Boston area.

Another historic walking tour is the Boston African American National Historic Site. It includes fifteen pre–Civil War structures relating to the city's African-American community, including the African Meeting House, the oldest standing African-American church in the United States.

The African Meeting House

An Artful City

Boston's architecture is a remarkable blend of old and new. The sixty-story John Hancock Tower, New England's highest skyscraper, stands behind Trinity Church, which was built more than a century ago. "You can see the reflection of the historic Trinity Church in the windows of the very modern John Hancock skyscraper. You can read about cutting-edge research performed at the Massachusetts Institute of Technology while sitting in the Old North Church. I love the contrasts of this city," remarks Craig Wong, a Boston University student. An elevator ride to the top of the Prudential Center provides breathtaking views of the city and beyond, while a stroll through the cobblestone streets of Beacon Hill takes you to a time gone by.

Boston's museums and galleries store the city's wealth of art and antiquities. The Museum of Fine Arts, the Isabella Stewart Gardner Museum, and the Institute of Contemporary Art are just a few places to see Renaissance paintings, Egyptian mummies, American folk art, and the latest in modern art and design. Newbury Street, in the city's Back Bay neighborhood, is lined with small galleries and shops.

New reflects old: Trinity Church's image appears in the mirrored windows of the John Hancock Tower in Boston.

At the New England Aquarium, you can see thousands of fish and sea animals, pat a sea lion on the ear, and visit with a colony of penguins. Located nearby on Museum Wharf, the Boston Children's Museum offers hands-on science exhibits. Also along this wharf is the Boston Tea Party Ship, a floating, full-scale replica of the original ship. Visitors are even allowed to hurl some tea off the side of the ship, just as the patriots did in 1773.

TEN LARGEST CITIES

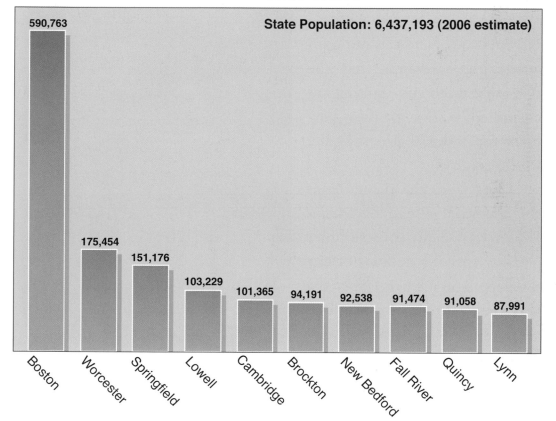

State Population: 6,437,193 (2006 estimate)

Boston 590,763
Worcester 175,454
Springfield 151,176
Lowell 103,229
Cambridge 101,365
Brockton 94,191
New Bedford 92,538
Fall River 91,474
Quincy 91,058
Lynn 87,991

The southern arm of Massachusetts Bay, known as the South Shore, is home to Plymouth. It was at Plymouth that the Pilgrims landed in 1620 to found the first permanent European settlement north of Virginia. Today, visitors can see Plymouth Rock and tour a replica of the *Mayflower*. On board, costumed guides portraying passengers describe the difficult journey across the Atlantic. Back on land, the National Monument to the Forefathers bears the names of the 102 *Mayflower* passengers.

Step back into seventeenth-century New England at Plimoth Plantation, a living history museum that re-creates the early Pilgrim town. Here you can learn about the hardships that the Pilgrims faced by talking to costumed guides as they perform the tasks of everyday life in the colony.

Cape Cod, the peninsula at the southeastern end of Massachusetts, is a favorite summer getaway spot for millions of city dwellers. The Upper Cape, the area closest to the mainland, is speckled with acres of cranberry bogs and small ponds, while the Lower Cape is known for its sand dunes and sunny beaches.

At Plimoth Plantation, children dress in period costume to illustrate what life was like for the Pilgrims.

INDIAN PUDDING

The Pilgrims' first few winters in the New World were rough, as food was scarce. One staple that the settlers had in abundance, thanks to help from local Native Americans, was corn. Pilgrims created this savory dessert using cornmeal as a base. You can make the same dessert yourself, with help from an adult. Just follow these easy directions.

    1/3 cup plus 1 tablespoon cornmeal
    4 cups whole milk
    1/2 cup molasses
    4 tablespoons unsalted butter
    2 tablespoons sugar
    1 1/2 tablespoons ground ginger
    1/2 teaspoon salt

Preheat the oven to 275 °F. Place the cornmeal in a large saucepan. Stir in the milk very slowly to avoid lumps. Stirring constantly, bring the mixture to a boil over medium heat and cook it for three minutes. Reduce the heat as low as possible and cook for fifteen minutes, stirring frequently. Remove the dish from heat. Then stir in the remaining ingredients.

Butter a 9-inch baking dish. Pour the mixture into it. Bake until the center looks firm but is still slightly quivery when the dish is shaken—make sure to use oven mitts! A dark crust will form on top. Let the dessert cool on a rack for thirty minutes to an hour. Then enjoy with a scoop of ice cream or a dollop of fresh whipped cream.

Colorful international flags flutter overhead as people walk, drive, or bike down Commercial Street in Provincetown.

Between the Upper Cape and the Lower Cape is Hyannis, known as the summer resort of the Kennedy family and the site of ferries that take passengers to Nantucket Island and Martha's Vineyard. Martha's Vineyard is a popular vacation area that attracts artists and celebrities—including former president Bill Clinton—to its pristine beaches. Nantucket's charm is associated with its cobblestone streets and quaint villages.

At the cape's farthest tip lies Provincetown, where the Pilgrims first landed before they settled in Plymouth. For such a small, isolated community, the town has a very cosmopolitan mix of people. The beachfront is serene and relaxing, while the town's two commercial streets are lined with discos, museums, shops, and a wide variety of restaurants. The attitude here is fun, open, and carefree—quite a contrast to the Puritan ethic that once dominated Massachusetts.

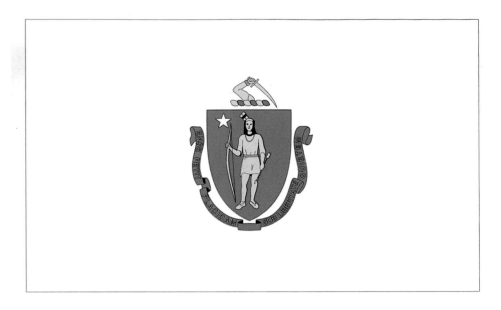

THE FLAG: The Massachusetts flag shows the shield that appears on the state seal against a white background.

THE SEAL: In the center of the Massachusetts state seal is a gold Indian on a blue shield. The Indian's arrow is pointing downward to show that he is peaceful. Above the Indian is a silver star, which indicates that Massachusetts was one of the original thirteen states. The arm holding a sword illustrates the state motto, which is written in Latin on the ribbon below the shield.

State Survey

Statehood: February 6, 1788

Origin of Name: From the Massachusetts, a Native-American tribe whose name means "near the great hill"

Nickname: Bay State

Capital: Boston

Motto: By the Sword We Seek Peace, but Peace Only under Liberty

Bird: Chickadee

Flower: Mayflower

Tree: American elm

Fish: Cod

Beverage: Cranberry juice

Dog: Boston terrier

Mayflowers

Boston terrier

MASSACHUSETTS

Arlo Guthrie composed this song in 1976. Massachusetts is the only state to have an official state folk song.

Words and Music by Arlo Guthrie

The sun comes up to meet the dawn, another day that must go on,
There's another night that's gone in Massachusetts.
And I could spend all of my days, and remain each day amazed
At the way each day is phrased in Massachusetts. Chorus

Now if you could only see, well I know you would agree,
There ain't nowhere else to be like Massachusetts.
And there's a house upon a hill that keeps us from the chill,
And by the Grace of God we will be in Massachusetts. Chorus

Horse: Morgan horse

Insect: Ladybug

Marine Mammal: Right whale

Mineral: Babingtonite

Stone: Granite

Dessert: Boston cream pie

GEOGRAPHY

Highest Point: 3,491 feet above sea level, at Mount Greylock

Lowest Point: sea level, along the Atlantic coast

Area: 8,262 square miles

Greatest Distance North to South: 113 miles

Greatest Distance East to West: 183 miles

Bordering States: Vermont and New Hampshire to the north; New York to the west; Connecticut and Rhode Island to the south

Hottest Recorded Temperature: 107 °F at New Bedford and Chester on August 2, 1975

Coldest Recorded Temperature: −34 °F at Birch Hill Dam on January 18, 1957

Average Annual Precipitation: 45 inches

Major Rivers: Blackstone, Charles, Chicopee, Concord, Connecticut, Deerfield, Hoosic, Housatonic, Merrimack, Millers, Mystic, Nashua, Neponset, Westfield

Major Lakes: Assawompsett, Long Pond, North Watuppa, Quabbin, Wachusett, Webster

Trees: ash, beech, birch, eastern hemlock, eastern white pine, maple, oak, pitch pine, red pine

Wild Plants: azalea, dogwood, marigold, mountain laurel, rhododendron, rush, sedge, skunk cabbage, trillium, viburnum, violet

Animals: beaver, chipmunk, copperhead snake, deer, fox, meadow mouse, muskrat, porcupine, rabbit, raccoon, right whale, skunk, squirrel, timber rattlesnake

Birds: eastern meadowlark, grebe, hawk, heron, partridge, pheasant, pileated woodpecker, purple martin, robin, sparrow, tern, warbler, wild turkey

Fish: bass, cod, flounder, haddock, pickerel, sunfish, swordfish, trout, tuna, white perch, whiting, yellow perch

Endangered Animals: American burying beetle, blue whale, dwarf wedgemussel, eastern puma, finback whale, hawksbill sea turtle, humpback whale, Kemp's ridley sea turtle, leatherback sea turtle, Plymouth redbelly turtle, Puritan tiger beetle, right whale, roseate tern, sei whale, shortnose sturgeon

Endangered Plants: northeastern bulrush, sandplain gerardia

The endangered American burying beetle

Massachusetts History

1500s Nauset, Nipmuc, Patuxet, Pocomtuc, and Wampanoag Native-American tribes live in the area.

1602 Bartholomew Gosnold becomes the first European known to land in present-day Massachusetts.

1620 The Pilgrims arrive at Plymouth.

1630 The Puritans found Massachusetts Bay Colony; Boston is founded.

1635 Boston Latin School, the first secondary school in the American colonies, is established.

1636 Harvard, the first college in the American colonies, is founded.

1640 The *Bay Psalm Book*, America's first English-language book, is published in Cambridge.

1676 Colonists defeat the Wampanoag tribe in King Philip's War.

1690 The American colonies' first newspaper, *Publick Occurrences Both Forreign and Domestick*, is established in Boston.

1692 Nineteen people are executed as a result of the Salem witch trials.

1770 British soldiers kill five colonists in the Boston Massacre.

1773 Colonists dump British tea into Boston Harbor during the Boston Tea Party.

1775 The American Revolution begins.

1780 The Massachusetts Constitution is adopted.

1788 Massachusetts becomes the sixth state in the Union.

1796 Bay Stater John Adams is elected second president of the United States.

1814 Francis Cabot Lowell begins the U.S. textile industry in Waltham by opening a mill where all the stages of cloth manufacturing take place.

1824 Bay Stater John Quincy Adams is elected sixth president of the United States.

1831 William Lloyd Garrison begins publishing his antislavery newspaper, the *Liberator*, in Boston.

1837 Mount Holyoke, the nation's first women's college, is established in South Hadley.

1852 Massachusetts becomes the first U.S. state to require children to attend school.

1861–1865 About 150,000 Bay Staters fight in the Civil War.

1876 Alexander Graham Bell invents the telephone in Boston.

1897 The nation's first subway begins operation in Boston.

1903 Baseball's first World Series is played in Boston.

1914–1918 World War I is fought.

1939–1945 World War II is fought.

1960 Massachusetts native John F. Kennedy is elected thirty-fifth president of the United States.

1974 Boston begins a busing program to desegregate its schools.

1980 Massachusetts voters pass Proposition 2 1/2, which drastically cuts property taxes.

1988 Massachusetts celebrates its two-hundredth anniversary as a state.

1991 The Big Dig begins.

2001 Advanced Cell Technology, a Massachusetts-based company, announces that it has created a human embryo clone.

2003 The underground highway replacing Boston's Central Artery opens.

2004 Same-sex marriage is legalized in Massachusetts; Senator John Kerry runs for president of the United States.

2007 Former governor Mitt Romney announces his candidacy for the U.S. presidency.

ECONOMY

Agricultural Products: apples, cranberries, eggs, greenhouse plants, maple syrup, milk, sweet corn

Manufactured Products: chemicals, computer and electrical equipment, fabricated metal products, musical instruments, noncomputer electronic machinery, paper and printed materials, plastic, rubber, toys and games, transportation equipment

Natural Resources: crushed stone, fish, granite, gravel, marble, sand

Business and Trade: banking and finance, education, high-technology research and development, medical care, real estate, tourism, wholesale and retail trade

CALENDAR OF CELEBRATIONS

Chinese New Year Boston marks the beginning of the Chinese calendar in January or February with lots of exploding firecrackers and a parade featuring long dancing serpents.

St. Patrick's Day Everyone is Irish on March 17, when Boston holds one of the nation's largest St. Patrick's Day parades.

Patriot's Day Many residents of Lexington and Concord get up early on this April morning, when the beginning of the American Revolution is reenacted. Men dressed as Paul Revere and other riders begin the festivities by galloping through the towns and shouting, "The Regulars [British soldiers] are out!"

World's Largest Pancake Breakfast For just three hours on a May morning in Springfield, 60,000 people sit down at a four-block-long table to eat their fill of pancakes served up by four hundred volunteers.

Tanglewood For more than two months beginning in late June, Lenox hosts one of the world's premiere classical music festivals. Hundreds of thousands of people enjoy symphonies, choral music, jazz, and other entertainment in the beautiful Berkshire Hills.

Boston Harborfest More than a million people attend six days of events in Boston in late June and early July. Highlights include a jazz concert, a fleet of tall ships sailing into Boston Harbor, a contest for the best New England clam chowder, and a spectacular Fourth of July fireworks display.

Lowell Folk Festival At this July festival, you might hear music ranging from Inuit singers to Vietnamese bands. In addition to all the music, you can attend parades, dances, and international crafts demonstrations.

Puerto Rican Day Parade In this July celebration, the Puerto Rican community of Holyoke hosts a large parade, lots of music, and a chance to celebrate Puerto Rican culture and traditions.

Caribbean Carnival The highlight of this August event in Boston is a parade filled with colorful costumes, elaborate floats, and huge steel-drum groups. You can also taste spicy Caribbean food.

Essex ClamFest Essex claims to have invented fried clams in 1916. Each September, the town honors its clam history at an event where you can eat clams fried or in fritters, cakes, or chowder. Pony rides, Dixieland jazz bands, and art exhibits help keep everyone entertained.

Cranberry Harvest Festival Each September, 200,000 people descend on Harwich to honor one of the state's most famous agricultural products. Visitors savor cranberry drinks, breads, muffins, and jellies while watching a parade.

Head of the Charles Regatta Boston hosts one of the world's largest rowing events each October. More than 4,500 rowers compete in events on the Charles River.

Thanksgiving Day On Thanksgiving day in November, feasts are held throughout Plymouth, the site of the first Thanksgiving. A parade, complete with marching bands and floats, tops off the festivities.

First Night On the last day of December, Boston celebrates the new year with music, dancing, mimes, ice sculptures, children's activities, and fireworks.

John Adams (1735–1826), of Braintree, was the second president of the United States. Before the American Revolution, Adams argued for independence when many colonial leaders were still trying to settle their differences with Britain. As a member of the Continental Congress, he pushed for the adoption of the Declaration of Independence. He also drafted the Massachusetts Constitution. His son, John Quincy Adams, was the nation's sixth president.

Louisa May Alcott (1832–1888) wrote the classic novel *Little Women*. This story of four sisters growing up in New England was based on her own life. Besides writing other classic family novels such as *Little Men* and *Jo's Boys*, Alcott wrote thrillers under a fake name in order to earn money. She grew up in Boston and Concord.

Crispus Attucks (1723?–1770), the first person killed in the American colonists' fight for freedom, died during the Boston Massacre. Little is known of Attucks's background, but many historians believe he was African-American.

Clara Barton (1821–1912) was born in Oxford. She became a teacher and established some of the first free schools in New Jersey. During the Civil War, Barton took supplies to soldiers and nursed the wounded. After the war, she organized a systematic search for missing soldiers. Congress eventually funded what became known as the Missing Soldiers Office, and Barton became the first woman to run a government bureau. In 1881, Barton created the American Red Cross to help victims of war and natural disaster. She served as the organization's president for more than twenty years.

John Adams

Leonard Bernstein (1918–1990) is a leading American conductor and composer. In 1943, Bernstein made his conducting debut with the New York Philharmonic. Fifteen years later, he became the first American director of the philharmonic and greatly increased its reputation. Although Bernstein composed operas and ballets, he is best remembered for his scores to the musicals *West Side Story* and *On the Town*. Bernstein was born in Lawrence.

Leonard Bernstein

Patricia Bradley (1951–   ), a native of Westford, is the only golfer to win three of the four major women's championships in a single season. Bradley joined the Ladies Professional Golf Association (LPGA) tour in 1974. Since then, she has been named LPGA Player of the Year twice and has won more than thirty titles. Bradley was the first female golfer to top $3 million in career earnings. She is a member of the LPGA Hall of Fame.

Anne Bradstreet (1612?–1692) was one of the first important American poets. She was born in Northampton, England, and moved to Massachusetts Bay Colony in 1630. Her collection *The Tenth Muse Lately Sprung Up in America*, the first book of poetry written in the American colonies, was published in 1650. Her best poems deal with the difficult lives of the settlers.

Edward Brooke (1919–   ) was the first African-American U.S. senator after Reconstruction, the period immediately following the Civil War. Brooke, who grew up in Washington, D.C., attended Boston University Law School. In 1962, he was elected attorney general of Massachusetts. As attorney general, he made nationwide headlines for exposing corruption in the state government. In 1966, Brooke, a Republican, was elected to the U.S. Senate, thus becoming the first black ever elected to the Senate by a popular vote.

Bette Davis (1908–1989), one of the greatest American movie actresses, was born in Lowell. She made her film debut in 1931 in *Bad Sister* and became a star in 1934 after playing a scheming waitress in *Of Human Bondage*. Davis often appeared in melodramatic movies and played willfully independent, intense, and eccentric characters. Her most famous films include *The Little Foxes* and *All About Eve*. Davis eventually earned ten Academy Award nominations—more than any other actress of her time—and won twice.

Geena Davis (1957–   ) is a popular actress known for playing amiable, funny, and offbeat characters. Her most famous role was in *Thelma and Louise*, in which she played one of two women who leave their humdrum lives behind as they run from the police. Davis won an Academy Award for Best Supporting Actress for her performance as a dog trainer in *The Accidental Tourist*. She was born in Wareham.

Ralph Waldo Emerson (1803–1882), a philosopher who led the transcendentalist movement, was born in Boston. His first book, *Nature*, explained the ideas behind transcendentalism. This philosophy is based on individual freedom and the view that personal spiritual experiences are superior to formal religion. Emerson was also active in the antislavery movement.

Fannie Farmer (1857–1915), a Boston native, was the first cook to use standard measurements in recipes. She directed the Boston Cooking School for eleven years and then founded Miss Farmer's School of Cookery, where the students were housewives rather than professional cooks. She wrote the first *Fannie Farmer Cookbook* in 1896.

Fannie Farmer (left)

William Lloyd Garrison (1805–1879), of Newburyport, was a leading antislavery activist. He published the influential antislavery newspaper the *Liberator* and helped found the American Anti-Slavery Society. He served as the society's president for more than twenty years. His speeches against slavery aroused great hatred in the South, and he received many death threats. Garrison also worked for women's rights, the rights of Native Americans, and peace.

William Lloyd Garrison

Robert Goddard (1882–1945) was a rocket scientist whose work lay the foundation for space exploration. As a child in Worcester, Goddard dreamed of sending rockets to the Moon and even to Mars at a time when no one else considered it possible. In 1926, he launched the first rocket using liquid fuel, and three years later he sent up the first rocket carrying instruments, such as a thermometer and a camera. Over the course of his career, he earned more than two hundred patents related to rocketry.

Nathaniel Hawthorne (1804–1864) was one of the greatest nineteenth-century American writers. Hawthorne was born in Salem, and much of his work criticizes the intolerance of his Puritan ancestors. His best-known novel, *The Scarlet Letter*, is about a woman condemned by Puritan society because she has a baby and refuses to name the father. His other books, such as *The House of the Seven Gables* and *Twice-Told Tales*, also confront ethical questions and explore the dark side of human nature.

Winslow Homer (1836–1910), of Boston, was an artist famous for his dramatic seascapes. Homer began his career as an illustrator for *Harper's Weekly* magazine. He later became known for his powerfully realistic paintings of nature.

John F. Kennedy (1917–1963), the youngest person ever elected president of the United States, was born in Brookline. Kennedy, a member of a prominent Massachusetts family, served as a U.S. representative and senator before being elected the nation's first Roman Catholic president. As president, he worked on civil rights legislation and promoted space exploration. He also backed an unsuccessful invasion of Cuba to overthrow its leader, Fidel Castro. Kennedy's youth and charisma gave the nation hope. His assassination in 1963 shocked the world.

John Kerry (1943–) Although he was born in Colorado, John Kerry is far more associated with Massachusetts. He graduated from Boston College Law School and went into private practice. In 1982, he was elected the state's lieutenant governor, and two years later he became a U.S. senator. He was reelected in 1990, 1996, and 2002. Kerry won the Democratic nomination for president in 2004 but lost to incumbent George W. Bush.

Jack Lemmon (1925–2001), a native of Boston, was an actor who became famous for playing worried, well-meaning men in a heartless world. After working on stage and in television, he made his film debut in 1954 in *It Should Happen to You*. The following year he won an Academy Award for Best Supporting Actor for *Mister Roberts*. His most famous films include *Some Like It Hot*, *The Apartment*, and *The Odd Couple*. Lemmon was nominated for eight Academy Awards.

Horace Mann (1796–1859), who was born in Franklin, is considered the father of American public education because he led the fight for mandatory free schools in the United States. As a member of the Massachusetts legislature, Mann helped establish the nation's first state board of education. After he was appointed secretary of the state board of education, he became the leading figure in promoting non-religious public education. He rallied public support for increasing teachers' pay and founded schools for training teachers.

Rocky Marciano (1923–1969), of Brockton, is the only undefeated heavyweight champion in boxing history. He began boxing while serving in the U.S. Army during World War II. Marciano became heavyweight champion in 1952. By the time he retired in 1956, he had a record of 49 and 0 with 43 knockouts. Marciano is considered one of the hardest punchers in boxing history.

Rocky Marciano

Massasoit (1580–1661) was a Wampanoag Indian who befriended the Pilgrims. In 1621, Massasoit made a peace treaty with the Pilgrims, and the agreement lasted throughout his life. The Pilgrims invited Massasoit and other Wampanoag to a feast that became the first Thanksgiving.

Sylvia Plath (1932–1963) was a poet and novelist from Boston whose troubled life was the source of many of her most moving works. Some of her best poems, which appear in a collection called *Ariel*, were written shortly before her suicide. Plath's novel *The Bell Jar* is a classic account of a young woman's breakdown.

Massasoit

Dr. Seuss (1904–1991), one of the world's most beloved children's authors, was born Theodor Seuss Geisel in Springfield. His richly imaginative stories are filled with outlandish creatures and clever rhymes. Dr. Seuss's classic books include *The Cat in the Hat*, *Horton Hears a Who*, *How the Grinch Stole Christmas*, and *Green Eggs and Ham*.

Squanto (1586?–1622) was a Patuxet Indian who helped the Pilgrims survive by teaching them how to farm, fish, and hunt in Massachusetts. Before the Pilgrims arrived in America, Squanto had been kidnapped by Englishmen and sold as a slave in Spain. He eventually escaped and made his way back to America in 1619. Squanto had learned English, so in addition to teaching the Pilgrims survival skills, he served as an interpreter.

Barbara Walters (1931–) is a television journalist famous for her revealing interviews with celebrities. Walters, who was born in Boston, began her television career as a producer. In 1961, she became a writer and researcher for NBC's *Today* show, and in 1974, she became the program's cohost. Two years later, ABC lured her to its studio with a one-million-dollar contract, which was a record amount of money at the time.

TOUR THE STATE

Boston Children's Museum A gigantic bottle of milk lets you know that you've reached one of Boston's most fun-filled sites. The museum's hands-on exhibits range from the Japanese House, where you take off your shoes and step into a two-story silk merchant's home in Japan, to a KidStage with state-of-the-art equipment that allows you to be in the spotlight.

Charlestown Navy Yard (Boston) The prize of this navy yard is the USS *Constitution*, which was built in 1794 and is the world's oldest warship that is still afloat. You can visit the ship's top deck and a museum filled with information about the ship's history.

Isabella Stewart Gardner Museum (Boston) One of the nation's best art museums, the Gardner Museum is filled with such treasures as Renaissance paintings and entire rooms transported from European mansions.

John F. Kennedy Library (Boston) This museum has exhibits and videos about the late president and the rise of the Kennedy family. Some of Kennedy's possessions are also on display.

Museum of Science (Boston) With its butterfly garden, crime-scene investigator laboratory, and rock garden made of petrified wood and puddingstone, this museum never lets anyone get bored.

Paul Revere House (Boston) This is the only seventeenth-century building still standing in Boston. The interior reflects how it looked when Paul Revere lived there from 1770 to 1800. Exhibits show some of Revere's possessions and silverwork.

African Meeting House (Boston) Built in 1806, this simple building is the oldest surviving African-American church in the country.

New England Aquarium (Boston) Get a close-up view of hundreds of fish, along with playful dolphins, sea lions, and other creatures at this waterfront aquarium.

Walden Pond (Concord) Writer Henry David Thoreau made this pond famous after living alone there for two years. The pond is still beautiful and peaceful. Visitors can see the site of Thoreau's cabin and learn about his stay.

Salem Witch Museum (Salem) Various displays, including a sound and light show, bring the strange events of the Salem witch hunt to life.

Cape Cod National Seashore (Eastham) Bikers, hikers, and sunbathers enjoy thousands of acres of dunes, beaches, marshes, and woods that stretch along Cape Cod.

Whaling Museum (Nantucket) Housed in an 1846 building that was originally a candle factory, this fascinating museum is filled with whaling artifacts, such as harpoons, a gigantic oil press, and a fabulous collection of items carved from baleen.

Basketball Hall of Fame (Springfield) You'll get the whole story of basketball at this museum—from the game's origins, when Springfield's James Naismith first threw a soccer ball into a peach basket, to stories about the game's greatest players.

Hancock Shaker Village (Pittsfield) This museum preserves twenty buildings built by the Shakers, a religious group known for its simple, elegant, and practical crafts and buildings. The village's highlight is a round stone barn, where one man standing in the center could feed fifty-four cows at once.

Mohawk Trail (Greenfield) This 63-mile road skirts fantastic mountain vistas, quaint villages, and some of the most spectacular autumn colors found anywhere.

Pilgrim Monument (Provincetown) This 250-foot-tall monument marks the spot where the Pilgrims first landed in America. An observation deck at the top provides a stunning view of the tip of Cape Cod.

Plimoth Plantation (Plymouth) Step back in time to 1627 at this re-creation of a Pilgrim village. Actors dressed in authentic costumes and speaking with seventeenth-century English accents go through the motions of daily life—shearing sheep, playing games, and building houses.

Southwick's Zoo (Mendon) This zoo has the largest collection of animals in New England, including rhinoceroses, camels, zebras, and giant tortoises. At the petting zoo, visitors say hello to llamas, deer, and farm animals.

Old Sturbridge Village (Sturbridge) Forty buildings from around New England have been moved to this 200-acre park to re-create an early nineteenth-century village. Demonstrations by artisans include blacksmithing, printing, barrel making, and shoe making.

FUN FACTS

Boston built the first subway system in 1897.

In Rockport there is a house built entirely out of newspaper.

The Fig Newton cookie is named after the Massachusetts town
of Newton.

The Boston University Bridge on Commonwealth Avenue is the only
place in the whole world where a boat can sail under a train that is
rumbling under a car that is moving under an overhead airplane.

The Volleyball Hall of Fame is located in Holyoke.

Dedham is home to the Museum of Bad Art.

Find Out More

If you would like to find out more about Massachusetts, look in your school library, local library, bookstore, or video store. You can also surf the Internet. Here are some resources to help you begin your search.

BOOKS

Denenberg, Barry. *So Far from Home: The Diary of Mary Driscoll, An Irish Mill Girl, Lowell, Massachusetts, 1847*. New York: Scholastic, 2003.

Gellerman, Bruce and Erik Sherman. *Massachusetts Curiosities: Quirky Characters, Roadside Oddities and Other Offbeat Stuff*. Guilford, CT: Globe Pequot, 2004.

Tsipis, Yanni. *Building Route 128*. Mount Pleasant, SC: Arcadia Publishing, 2003.

MOVIES

Massachusetts: Discoveries America. Bennett-Wade Media, 2006.

Weekend Explorer: Cape Cod. Travel Video Store, 2005.

Mass.gov
http://www.mass.gov/
This is the official Web site of the State of Massachusetts. You can learn about history, government issues, cities and towns, and tourist sites.

Massachusetts: It's all here.
http://www.massvacation.com/
Learn about attractions and fun activities in the Bay State. Take a tour of Massachusetts history and trivia. Find out about the state's history and learn fun facts.

Famous American Trials: Salem Witchcraft Trials, 1692
http://www.law.umkc.edu/faculty/projects/ftrials/salem/salem.htm
Learn about the fascinating Salem Witch Trials.

Index

Page numbers in **boldface** are illustrations and charts.

Suzanne LeVert, an author of many books for children and young adults, was raised in Rockport, Massachusetts. For more than ten years she lived in Boston, soaking up the city's history, culture, architecture, and natural beauty.

Tamra B. Orr is the author of more than a hundred nonfiction books for people of all ages. She wishes she had as much time to read as she does to write and keeps collecting books for when that day comes. Orr writes testing material for various national tests, as well as books that help prepare test takers. She is mom to four charming kids and partner to one charming husband.